When Philosophers Rule

Commentaries by Ficino on Plato's Writings
a four-volume series

Gardens of Philosophy
Evermore Shall Be So
When Philosophers Rule
All Things Natural

When Philosophers Rule

FICINO ON PLATO'S
REPUBLIC, *LAWS*, and *EPINOMIS*

ARTHUR FARNDELL

SHEPHEARD-WALWYN (PUBLISHERS) LTD

First published in 2009 by
Shepheard-Walwyn (Publishers) Ltd
15 Alder Road
London SW14 8ER

British Library Cataloguing in Publication Data
A catalogue record of this book
is available from the British Library

ISBN: 978-0-85683-257-4

Typeset by Alacrity,
Sandford, Somerset
Printed and bound through
s|s|media limited, Wallington, Surrey

CONTENTS

ACKNOWLEDGEMENTS

MY WIFE, Phyllis, again heads the list. She has been a constant presence throughout the development of this book, giving encouragement, asking questions, and making suggestions. When the time came to consider the title, the three words instantly leapt from her mouth. Could any author ask for a better wife?

John Meltzer has given unfailing support; Christophe Poncet has supplied source material; Nathan David has graciously allowed images of his sculptures to be used; Jean Desebrock has crafted the beautiful layout; and Anthony Werner, as publisher, has moulded the whole work with intelligence and sensitivity. It is a pleasure to be able to acknowledge these fine people and their respective skills.

Special thanks go to Ian Mason for his willingness to write a foreword to this work.

Arthur Farndell

TRANSLATOR'S NOTE

AS PART OF his commentary to the Eighth Book of the *Republic* Ficino wrote an 'Exposition on Nuptial Number'. His exposition is not included in this volume. The interested reader is directed to Professor Michael J.B. Allen's *Nuptial Arithmetic: Marsilio Ficino's Commentary on the Fatal Number in Book VIII of Plato's Republic*, published in 1994 by the University of California Press.

FOREWORD

FREEDOM, as the medieval English lawyer Sir John Fortescue once observed, is a thing with which the nature of man has been endowed by God. Therefore, he said, wherever it is oppressed it strives of its own energy always to return.

Living as we do in an age in which freedom seems relatively secure for many people in democratic states, it is easy to lose sight of the foundations upon which lasting freedom is built. Such foundations have long antecedents as this volume demonstrates, it being a translation of commentaries written more than five hundred years ago on works that were written over two thousand five hundred years ago. Yet Plato's *Republic* and *Laws,* and these commentaries on them, remain as relevant today as they have ever been, examining as they do the necessary conditions for a successful society which offers civil freedom under the rule of law to all its citizens.

Central to Plato's view of civil society is *arete*, justice or righteousness. Our own age is full of calls for justice in all social and civil spheres, but what is common to these calls is an apparent view that justice is something that is dispensed by the state, its institutions and courts of law to otherwise deprived citizens. Justice has become a commodity which purports to right wrongs and compensate victims who have nothing to do themselves but register their complaint with the appropriate authorities.

Plato's view, endorsed by Ficino, is very different. For them justice is a state of the soul over which every man and woman has personal command. It is an orderly state of the inner being which is cultivated by good practice of other virtues: wisdom, temperance and courage, which combined in one person produce that state of being that is called just. There is nothing to be gained from looking for this from some external source.

The great value of Plato's works and these commentaries on them is that they require us to look again at the basis of the freedoms we enjoy in modern democratic societies. They warn us that democratic

ix

freedoms are not attained, or maintained, without effort and that those efforts involve every citizen coming to an understanding of their own role in securing justice in the state to which they belong. It is clear from this view that the best form of government is self-government, and that such government involves the citizen in taking command of his or her own inner life, developing the personal strength to control, direct and restrain their own appetites while bringing their soul under the rule of wisdom or reason so that it becomes a thing of order and beauty reflecting the goodness of God and showing itself to be such in their conduct towards others and towards the state.

It was this idea of inner, personal government that lay behind the English common lawyers' idea of the reasonable man, the free and lawful man of the English common law. Such a person was presumed to know the law because the law was nothing else but reason, and reasonable conduct was sufficient to keep the individual within the law. This conception, which still informs the many common law jurisdictions that followed the British around the globe, is the key to the successful development of free democratic states. The lessons reflected in the pages of this volume offer a guide for modern statesmen and citizens alike.

For Plato, democracy as described by him is a dangerous and delicate form of government amounting at its worst to little more than mob rule based on the primacy of the pleasure-loving appetites in the souls of the citizens. When this becomes dominant in the majority of citizens, the very foundations of participatory forms of government are destroyed as fewer and fewer people develop in themselves the virtues necessary for the government of themselves or of states. New laws are passed on a whim to demonstrate to electorates that their governors are dealing with the latest crisis, but without any real regard to the effect of such laws on the body politic. There is an inevitable tendency for citizens to become ever more dependent on the state for the regulation of every aspect of life; regulations multiply and the people, far from becoming free citizens, become instead ever more dependent on the ever-increasing bounty of the state to provide for every aspect of life. In the end this cannot be sustained because the state has to appropriate more and more of the wealth of its citizens in order to pay for the services which the citizens demand in exchange for their votes.

Plato sees descent into tyranny as the inevitable outcome of such a state of affairs. However, he also writes: 'Until philosophers are kings, or the kings and princes amongst men have the spirit and power of philosophy, cities will have no rest from their evils, or so I believe.'

This is the opening that offers hope that the otherwise inevitable descent of democratic societies first into ungovernableness and then into tyranny can be avoided. In a democratic age, the kings and princes amongst men are the people themselves. The turning to philosophy that avoids the descent into tyranny is a revolution in personal values and an acceptance of personal responsibility. The free and lawful person acts reasonably and governs him or her self, not only because it is necessary for the good of the state and their neighbours, but also because such self-command offers greater happiness and fulfilment to the individual. Understanding this and making it a practical reality is necessary to the establishment and continuance of democratic governance based on freedom under law.

When the governors of a state understand this, following Plato, they are more likely to direct their lawmaking powers to establishing and maintaining virtue in the souls of the citizens and the citizens will appreciate and applaud their efforts to do so.

This volume is the first translation into English of Ficino's *Commentaries* on Plato's two greatest works on this topic. The *Commentaries* are themselves full of additional insights which expand and elucidate Plato's thought. They provide the modern reader with a route into an art and science of government which can offer both personal development and also the peace, freedom and stability to which modern democracies aspire. Perhaps the appearance of this translation at this time is a part of that volition described by Fortescue by which the real freedom of the human condition re-asserts itself from age to age.

Ian Mason
Principal, School of Economic Science

PART ONE

The Commentary of Marsilio Ficino to Plato's *Republic*

The Theme of the
First Book of the *Republic*

AS THE EYE surpasses the hand, the head the feet, reason the senses, the soul the body, the end all that is directed towards the end, stillness movement, and eternity time, so the contemplative life is seen to surpass the active life. For contemplation is the beginning and end of action: it directs action as it wills and it brings action to a stop, commanding the lesser movements and external action to cease, so that the inner, steadfast and freer action may at length be controlled. Thus, from the very contemplation of God all the movements and actions of the heavens and of nature are guided as if from their inception to their end.

It is for this reason that our Plato surpasses all other founders of States and lawgivers in this respect at least, that while all the others, as human beings, have organised the State mainly for action, Plato, as if divine, guides the entire activity – both public and private – of the State mainly towards contemplation and establishes his State as the mistress of the world, not that it may be feared by many but rather that it may be reverenced by all peoples as the heavenly Jerusalem fully manifest on earth, a State from which all disputes concerning possession have been removed and all things are common to all in accordance with the law of nature. Abundance is universal, harmony is firmly established, the will of all is single, and thus the tranquillity needed for contemplation is always readily available.

Now he assembles the entire form of the ideal Republic within ten books, the number which is the most wholesome of all numbers, for it contains other numbers within itself and it reproduces other numbers endlessly from itself. And, as he frequently declares in these books, especially in the second, he prefers us to record the entire discussion as a discussion about justice rather than about a Republic, teaching thereby, as I judge, that every situation and every action, both public and private, should be related not to abundance, not to power, and not to victory, but to justice herself. For once all disturbances have been removed and all hindrances caused by disputes have been banished,

3

justice herself renders the citizens fully prepared for the investigation of truth and the worship of God.

It is this kind of contemplation and worship that our Plato considers to be the specific aim of the Republic; so that, just as no one, whether living alone or in a community, can act without the law, in the same way many citizens, gathered together into the single body of the State by a common law, may fulfil this aim. *Timaeus* and *Critias* teach us, moreover, that before the great flooding of the lands Athens existed in a different form; and according to the Greeks and the Egyptians it was governed by laws similar to theirs.

It was the goddess Pallas who founded Athens, nurtured it and taught it and gave it the form of a Republic which Plato describes in his books. But in the books of the *Laws* he composes the State on the model of the government of Crete, Sparta, and the new Attica, and he begins the work with God, the author of all laws.

But let us return to what is in hand: he begins this State, too, with favourable auspices, the holy ceremonies of divine wisdom, the traditions and counsels of the elders, and the justice and holiness of religion. For after saying that to God should be rendered prayers and to every man his own, he begins with a discussion of private justice and will thus move, when it is appropriate, to public justice in its turn. Yet you are to remember that what is meant by Plato in these considerations is that without justice, divine and human, without the counsel of the elders, and without the grace of divine wisdom, no State can be happily established or, if established, be happily governed.

Next, touching on the theme of the first book, I shall select, from a host of weighty precepts, a few essential ones. Restrained youth makes for an easy old age, unrestrained youth for a difficult old age. He who complies with the lusts of the body is undoubtedly a slave to frenzied tyrants. In old age, now that the disturbances which youth brings in its train have abated, the soul, being separated from the body, looks more closely and more openly upon things divine. Blamelessness alone offers the soul the best hope for the future, the only solace of life. The man of sound mind will deem that money is useful for this above all, that he may discharge whatever he has vowed to God or promised to man or owes in any other way, and that he may not be led, on account of poverty, to lie to anyone or to be deceitful in any matter. For money should be related to justice, while justice should be related to the reward of another life.

But before we pursue the discussion about justice, my advice is to consider individual matters that are dealt with allegorically by Plato. Firstly, the old man Cephalus, the 'head', provides the starting-point for the discussion. Secondly, Polemarchus is the chief, which is what his name means: that is, he is the first to enter the fray in a restrained manner. Thirdly, Thrasymachus, the 'fierce fighter', acts harshly. Socrates, however, the 'powerful saviour', rescues everyone everywhere from error and from injustice.

But leaving allegory for the commentaries, let us now proceed to the definition of justice. Simonides, Pittacus, and Bias are reported to have said that justice is speaking the truth and rendering to each his due. Some interpret this to mean simply disclosing the truth to anyone and restoring what you have taken. But Socrates rejects this on the grounds that the full truth should not be revealed to a madman, or weapons returned to him which he had left in your keeping while he was of sound mind.

Others expound justice as giving to each what is meet for him: benefit to friends, but deprivation to enemies; assistance to the good, but harm to the wicked. Socrates rejects this definition, too, on the grounds that it is never right to harm anyone. For whoever harms anything makes it weaker and less fitting for its own work and detracts from its specific excellence, just as someone who harms a dog makes it unable to achieve canine excellence. But justice is the excellence of man, and so whoever harms a man makes him weaker in relation to justice. Yet justice never detracts from justice, just as music never destroys the work of music. This is why it is not just to harm anyone.

At this point Thrasymachus raises an objection against Socrates, as many others do at other times, because he will never answer but always wishes to ask. However, you cannot be unaware that there are many reasons why Socrates is always in the habit of asking questions rather than giving instruction.

The first reason is to remind the presumptuous that, whatever one's age, it is better to learn than to teach.

The second reason is to show that, by divine inspiration, truth is immediately showered upon minds which through appropriate questioning have been detached from the body and from errors, a situation which meets with the full approval of Avicenna.

The third reason is to make it clear that the forms of things have been implanted in our souls, and it is through these forms that the truth of things always suffuses souls which are turned towards them through the process of questioning.

The fourth reason is to make it clear that human knowledge consists in negating what is false rather than in affirming what is true.

The next definition of justice to be brought forward, similar to that of Callicles in *Gorgias*, is the one given by Thrasymachus, that what is just is what is advantageous to the more powerful; for those who are more powerful always exercise sovereignty, bring in laws that are advantageous to themselves, and rule over those that are subject to them; indeed, their subjects act justly when they obey those laws which have been established for the advantage of the rulers. Socrates opposes Thrasymachus, for how can a leader, through ignorance, prescribe those laws which will be to his own detriment? If a subject keeps those laws he will be just because he is obeying his lord, but he will also be unjust because he is acting to the disadvantage of his lord.

He adds that when any art which is fully fledged and therefore without defect is dealing with objects or people it looks not to its own advantage but to the advantage of whatever has been entrusted to it, as can be seen with a tutor and his pupils, a doctor and those who are sick, or a helmsman and the sailors; and in the same way a rightful magistrate looks to the advantage of those who are subject. But if any art, such as the art of medicine, exacts a payment, it is not medicine (whose end is the healing of disease) insofar as it makes a profit, but it is entangled with gain and prostitution. The art of civil government, therefore, being the most complete of all the arts and thus suffering from no defect or meanness, undoubtedly governs without seeking any advantage for itself.

I pass over what Thrasymachus rashly, and with some inconsistency, brings forward against justice. But you should note that it is not right for anyone to seek leadership or to solicit the magistracy. Again, if a State of good men ever exists, they will vie for the position of not ruling, in the same way that men nowadays strive out of a desire to rule.

But there are three things to note now. The first is that evil men are not to be admitted to the magistracy. The second is that citizens who are not evil are not to be encouraged, by the inducement of some reward or honour, to shoulder the heavy burden of governing. The third is that upright men, who are not moved by greed or ambition, must not be summoned to the State merely at a time of danger or fear, lest they themselves be subjected to the unjust government of worse men.

The divine Plato understands that at any time the duty of governing the country must be undertaken voluntarily if it is to be just. But by the example of the most upright citizen he wishes to reprove the unjust arrogance of those who in any way seek the magistracy from ambition or go hunting for honours. But men become worthy of honours by having not the least care for them.

He therefore wishes such an office to be undertaken voluntarily and at the same time to be necessary, so that the most upright man will most willingly take the helm of State, but he will do so only when necessity demands, and in the meantime he will prefer contemplation to action. Yet whenever the situation is urgent he will, to suit the occasion, put action on behalf of the public good before his personal contemplation. All of this can be very clearly understood from Plato's letter to Archytas of Tarentum.

After this comes the refutation of the tyrannical statement made by Thrasymachus, which allocates justice to the category of foolishness and evil, while allocating injustice to the category of wisdom and goodness. His statement is shown to be false on the grounds that every art is a sort of wisdom and that, in relation to those things concerning which it is wise, it is also good. However, a man who is skilled in any art does not seek more than another who is skilled in this art, but he seeks to obtain something equal or similar. Yet although he does not wish to rival the skilled man, he does wish to rise above the unskilled. But the unskilled man sometimes tries recklessly to arrogate to himself more than the skilled and the unskilled have together.

Very similar to the skilled man is the just man, who wishes to have nothing more than another just man, but something – namely, virtue – more than the unjust man. On the other hand, the unjust man, like the unskilled man, strives to have more than the just and the wicked have together.

The conclusion against Thrasymachus is that justice is to be referred to the category of wisdom and goodness, while injustice is to be referred to the category of folly and evil. Added to this is the fact that injustice is the cause of weakness for all people, since, in any society, injustice, begetting hatred and discord, completely undermines the society and finally destroys it.

A society can hold together only to the extent that some just distribution is maintained. It therefore stands by justice and is destroyed by injustice. Through justice it is a friend to itself and to others; through injustice it is an enemy to all. But the effects of justice and injustice upon a society are the same as their effects upon the soul: the just man is at harmony with himself, and he is a friend to himself, to all men, and to the gods; for the gods are most just, and thus it is not surprising that the just man is like them and is their friend. The unjust man, however, finds that his situation is the opposite in all respects.

Moreover, everything has its specific way of working and needs a specific talent or faculty which allows it to function at its best and without which it cannot be effective. Therefore, since the soul has something specific to care for and govern, and much more importantly to keep alive, she requires her own specific power to fulfil these functions most efficiently; and if this be removed, she struggles. Now the virtue of the soul is justice, and injustice is her vice. And so it is through justice that she gives perfect care and government, and that she lives, and lives happily. But if justice be taken away, the reverse is true.

Once these points have been stated, the first book concludes with a mild rebuke: although the definition and nature of justice should, of course, have been propounded earlier, what has happened so far is the opposite, as Socrates has followed those participating in the discussion and has, at the same time, while pursuing the debate according to well-known principles, taken into account the aptitude of those listening and has given due consideration to their capacity.

The Theme of the
Second Book of the *Republic*

THE SECOND BOOK begins with the threefold division of good things. The Good is unchanging and should be sought. Now we seek something for its own sake when we look for pleasures and happiness. We seek something for the sake of something else when we look for anything that is toilsome. We seek something for its own sake and for something other when we look for knowledge and good health.

Plato says that justice is to be sought for the sake of the others who benefit from it, and particularly for its own sake. But before a full definition of justice can be given, Glaucon pursues – at some length, with some fine distinctions, and with some restraint – those points which Thrasymachus passed over in his support of injustice. For he says – not because this is his view but because he wishes to spur Socrates into making a more vigorous defence of justice – that he is going to praise injustice. We find a similar situation in *Gorgias*.

Then Adeimantus speaks in support of justice, attributing to it benefits both human and divine. Here you will mark some of the sacred mysteries of the poets. Next he brings forward certain things as evidence to support injustice, referring to the persons of Socrates and Thrasymachus, and adding that he himself does not wish to vilify injustice but wishes to provoke Socrates somehow or other. However, he wishes to hear justice praised, not for her external trappings but for her intrinsic nature, in ways that others have not followed.

But you should take note that Plato has again put forward here many points relating to poets and priests; and not without good cause, for when he is mocking the superstitions of the people he shows that the licence to sin takes its rise frequently from poets and even more frequently from bad priests. Nor is it without some reason that Plato has introduced into these books, which are the dearest of all to him, the persons who are dearest to his heart: his brothers, Glaucon and Adeimantus, and his father, Ariston.

Note, too, that throughout his life Socrates, setting aside external impressions, found nothing more worthy of contemplation than to inquire into the nature and activity of virtue and vice within the soul, as he will show, of his own accord and later when prompted, in relation to justice and injustice.

But I myself have now acted most unjustly in failing to mention that reward of justice which is deduced from the thoughts of Musaeus and which he calls a state of constant inebriation. Musaeus himself received the idea from Orpheus, who expressed it through the sacred rites of Dionysus. It reminds us of the words of the prophet: I shall be drunk 'with the fatness of thy house'.

Drunkenness is thus of two kinds. The first kind is under the influence of the Moon and is caused by drinking the waters of Lethe, so that the mind, being put outside itself and beneath itself, forgets things divine and staggers about in the trammels of earthly things. The second kind is above the influence of the Moon and is caused by a draught of nectar, so that the mind, being put outside itself and above itself, forgets mortal infirmities and in absorbing matters divine is dazzled by their primal brilliance; or rather, by savouring their taste, is taken out of its old ways by some unfamiliar warmth. But soon the mind sees clearly, enjoys wholesome tastes, and is properly nourished.

Indeed, the divine Idea, by which the mind was made, penetrates the mind when it returns, as flavour penetrates taste. Its first action is to gently wash from the mind all that is foreign to it. Then it fills the mind completely, giving it greater delight by so doing. Its third action is to bring the mind back to itself, flooding it with inexpressible joy, when the mind first becomes intellect through the soul and finally becomes God through the intellect. And it no longer savours as it previously did, but it savours new things in a new way. And just as, in our experience, a strong imagination forms and moves the body, so in that realm the body together with its senses, being subject to the soul, is directly moved and shaped by the powerful action of the mind, so that body and senses are wondrously soothed by the ineffable sweetness of the mind.

But let us now revert to the subject of justice. Socrates hunts for justice in one thing after another as the end and object of his discussion, but because it is difficult to find it in the mind he looks for it first of all in the State, believing that it will be easier to see it there; and thus it is by reference to the State that he eventually defines, with clarity, the justice of the soul. Yet for him to be able to consider justice within the State, he formed the State at the outset, declaring at first the nature of its origin or corresponding need; then the nature of its substance or its necessary materials and arts; and finally its form or rule of life and its lawful government.

And we can see the praise he allots to the temperate life, the life that is healthy and adequate, and the scorn he reserves for the life of pleasure and self-indulgence, the life of unhealthiness and enormous want, which spawns war and makes the presence of soldiers a necessity in a State of this kind. This is why, when he comes to the careful arrangements for military service, he is meticulous in his provision of whatever is necessary for a vigorous soldier and guardian of the State.

But in all these matters remember that it is impossible for any one person to be born equipped for a variety of functions, and that, for this reason, no single person should practise divergent professions, especially since the work done by one person may be hindered by the work of another. Each person should rather practise a specific art from childhood and pursue it unceasingly throughout life. A soldier, furthermore, is born to be the guardian of his country, and he should be trained so that, like a dog, he is gentle towards those he knows, but towards those he does not know he is fierce, ever vigilant, and alert.

Socrates is thus stating that the beginning of any undertaking is of the utmost importance, especially for those of tender years, when both aspects are easily moulded. This is why he is right to shape the soldiers of the future from their infancy, training their minds through music and their bodies through gymnastic. Music includes those stories of the poets which he carefully prescribes for the ears of children and which alone will, like games, inspire and instruct them in the military art. And in a similar way he directs that others become familiar, from their childhood, with those stories which are most conducive to their future occupation. All other stories he keeps far away from them. This is his most important directive.

He then expresses his abhorrence of poetical impiety, which fabricates disgraceful stories about the gods, and he forbids tales of this type to be heard.

He adds two aspects of theology. The first is that God is good in all respects and is the cause of good things only and never the cause of anything evil. If God punishes anyone, it is for the sake of the Good. The second aspect is that God is totally unchanging, for He is the fullness of simplicity, power, excellence, and wisdom. And so he denies that God ever deceives anyone with untrue images, signs, or words. For God does not assume various forms, and since He does not change He does not feign change.

Let us conclude this book with some golden statements. A lie is the most hateful of all things in the eyes of gods and men. If falsehood in speech is hateful and is an expression of falsehood in the mind, it is undoubtedly true that falsehood in the mind is extremely hateful in the sight of gods and men. This kind of falsehood is ignorance, which causes the mind to deceive itself about the truth of things. But since truth looks upon that which is said to be, while untruth deviates towards non-being, it follows that the further a man of lies falls into falsehood, the further he slips into nothingness.

The Theme of the
Third Book of the *Republic*

THE THIRD BOOK takes further the training of the guardians that was begun in the second book. And just as, in the second book, he forbade them to hear false or base things about the gods, so now he forbids them to hear words of tragedy about the inhabitants of the underworld, words which might make them somewhat apprehensive. He also forbids them to hear words of comedy which might provoke laughter on an immoderate scale; for the man who is frequently reduced to tears through excessive laughter becomes as soft as the man who is brought to tears through sorrow. But since the guardians are to be kept well away from cowardice as well as from intemperance, greed, and injustice, he also forbids them to hear poetical compositions which fabricate the lusts, ravages, and injustices allegedly perpetrated by gods, heroes, and great men.

Now this military training is the same in all respects for all the citizens.

Note here what he says about lying. Within a State lies are disastrous, when individuals lie to each other, and particularly when they lie to the magistrates. This is equivalent to lies told by the sick to their doctor or by sailors to the helmsman. However, in the interests of general safety, helmsmen themselves are allowed to be deceitful on occasions; and purely to prevent very serious harm from befalling someone, it is right for one individual to lie to another. It is also permissible to speak, with due measure, about ancient events whose truth is unknown and to portray through images those things of which we have no clear-cut conception.

He accordingly divides speech into three types: a simple account, a simple imitation, and a mixture of the two. But he condemns all talk which indiscriminately relates anything utterly worthless and throws a man into confusion. For anyone who industriously imitates something for a long time enters into its nature. This is why he directs the poet who gives harrowing portrayals of troubled souls, and who is thus harmful to the youth, to change his style and follow a pattern of steadiness, or else go far away from the city. He also says that the man who imitates or initiates a great number of things eventually falters in all of them, one by one, and becomes proficient in none of them.

12

Then he moves forward from the first kind of music, which is poetry, to the second kind, which he divides into three types: rhetoric, harmony, and rhythm. To begin with, he says that musicians give the name *phthongus* to that harmonious sound which is neither so low that the singer cannot go lower nor so high that the same singer cannot go higher. Then from such sounds he builds harmony, an agreeable measure achieved by an increase and decrease in the low notes, the high notes, and the intermediate notes.

There are four notes under consideration: the high note, the low note, the rising note, and the falling note. Again, there are four primary proportions: the double, which arises between two and one; the sesquialteral, between three and two; the sesquitertial, between four and three; and the sesquioctaval, between nine and eight. The harmony of the eighth note follows the double proportion; the harmony of the fifth note follows the sesquialteral; that of the fourth follows the sesquitertial; and finally the tone follows the sesquioctaval. But we have written more fully about these matters elsewhere.

In the third place comes rhythm, a particular order of movement and time, as can be seen from the second book of the *Laws*. For when you have reconciled the notes through a harmonious measure of increase and decrease brought about by tightening and loosening, there is a need for rhythm, by which you can measure the movements and times of the high notes, the low notes, and the intermediate notes, each by itself and each in relation to the others. I am referring to movements which are gentler or brisker, as well as to those which are intermediate, and to times which are longer, shorter, and equal, with intonations that are also long, short, and intermediate. Note that 'base' is a different word, which, according to its context, can mean foundation, seat, weight, development, or end.

Consideration should also be given to the nine most common levels of harmony and disharmony. The first level is in reason, which is opinion in harmony with the actual truth of the matter. Its opposite is false opinion, which is contrary to the truth. The second level is in imagination: its harmony is the orderly pursuit of reason, while its disharmony is the pursuit of externals. The third level is in the mode of operation, which either follows reason in a restrained way or follows imagination without restraint. The fourth level is in speech, which is noble when it follows the true path of reason, and ignoble when it follows the haphazard ways of the imagination. The fifth level is in song, whose harmony lies in imitating noble speech and whose disharmony lies in imitating ignoble speech. The sixth level is in sound, which can imitate either the first kind of song or the second kind. The seventh level is in the dainty step or the clumsy step related to dance. The eighth level is in the disposition of the limbs and of the whole body, a disposition which is as pleasing to look at as it is ready for gymnastic exercise. The ninth level is in those skilful operations of any art which accord with musical proportion.

These nine levels may remind you of the nine Muses. But remember that the finest harmony of all is the tempering of the mind, a harmony which is imitated by all those that follow and is enhanced when they are observed in their turn. This accounts for his directive that only those harmonies should be practised, heard, and observed which recall the steadfast condition of the mind which is not puffed up with pride, swept away by anger, softened and slackened by pleasure, broken by sorrow, or filled with complaints arising from affliction or want.

He thus approves of harmony that is deep and steady, and he disapproves of the extremes of vehemence and softness. He condemns complexity and praises simplicity before all else. He believes in particular that harmony exercises power over the soul, for the soul is a kind of divine harmony and is attuned, at times, to the celestial harmony, as Plato might say.

Again, the body consists of a kind of harmony, and it is by harmony that the spirit is given form. Moreover, the airy harmony of notes, which penetrates the airy spirit with its motion and conveys the emotion and soul of the singer, moves the emotion of the hearer by means of emotion, stirs the soul of the hearer by means of the soul, and is gradually instilled into his character.

In all these matters notice the very great care, both civil and religious, with which Plato provides instruction for his State, and, as he also shows in the *Statesman*, the way in which he always combines temperance with courage. Finally, he considers erotic pleasures to be base and inharmonious, and this is why he keeps them quite distinct from rightful love, which always yearns only for what is beautiful and harmonious.

He deals at length with music and gymnastic, for they are of the greatest importance: all men devote their energies to these two, and it is their duty to do so. For music wondrously strengthens and orders the mind and the spirit, while gymnastic does the same for the body in service of the mind. He adds that a good mind does not arise from a good body, but a good body is produced from a good mind.

14

He further adds that simple music enhances the health of the mind, while a simple diet promotes the health of the body; and, conversely, complex music and a complex diet are injurious to both. He says that when men lived temperate lives they had no need of physicians. He condemns narrow-minded ways of safeguarding the body as far as diet and treatments are concerned, and he says that if a State needs the painstaking care of doctors and judges this is a clear sign that it is badly organised.

He speaks of the functions of the doctor and the judge; and he chooses for a judge a good and sensible old man with experience of many types of people both good and evil. He describes depravity as a kind of deprivation which knows neither itself nor virtue; and he speaks of virtue as a way of life which knows itself through itself and which, when acquaintance with situations is added to it, makes judgements about vices.

It should always be remembered, however, that Plato confirms – not only in this dialogue but also in the *Laws*, the *Statesman*, and *Protagoras* – that there is nothing more needful to any man, especially to a public figure and a philosopher, than the bond which joins courage and temperance together as equal partners, so that, through courage the heights are sought, while through temperance the depths are not despised, and through the operation of them both you are never over-bold or over-fearful.

Through courage, again, you will ward off injury both private and public, and through temperance you will yourself abstain from injury. Through courage you will be summoned to all that is honourable, and through temperance you will be restrained from all that is base.

This is why he relates gymnastic and music to these two virtues, so that through the first may be acquired courage, mental rather than physical. He orders them to be blended together, since gymnastic in isolation begets ferocity, while music in isolation produces softness, and both together give rise to courage and temperance.

Finally, from those who have received such training he selects the guardians, or magistrates, and the defenders, or soldiers. Those he wishes to be taken up for the magistracy are those who are elderly, well-balanced, and brave, lovers of the public weal, those who have proved themselves such in experience.

Again, he directs the young men to be tested in the midst of pleasures and pains, in order to see whether or not they are temperate and courageous and whether, through deceits or threats or enticements, they might at any time be persuaded to deviate from their view of pre-serving the public good.

Lastly, he says that the temperaments of men are like different metals, gold being fit to govern, silver ready to be a soldier, and iron and bronze suitable for craftsmanship and agriculture. He decrees that individual talents be directed to those functions for which they are fitted; and thus the sons of the helmsmen should at times be directed to what is baser, in accordance with their talents, and the sons of the lower ranks should, in turn, be likewise directed to nobler functions.

He also forbids the soldiers to have any private property: this is to ensure that they do not, through greed, change from guard-dogs into wolves.

The Theme of the
Fourth Book of the *Republic*

IN THE FOURTH BOOK we hear of the measure that is applied to ownership and to the State to ensure that there are no excessively rich citizens and no poor citizens. For he thinks that uprisings occur and the State is destroyed from excessive abundance as well as from scarcity. He considers, too, that there is no unity, but rather division, in a State where some are poor while others are rich; and, as usually happens, the rich despise the poor, and the poor feel envy and hatred for the rich. From here he moves cautiously to his secret teaching that all things are common: none has less than any other, and none has more, for the first situation breeds envy, lying, and theft, while the second spawns extravagance, haughtiness, and sloth. Furthermore, possessing too much or too little is an obstacle to good character and harmony, as well as to talent and the arts. He teaches that the State is protected and undertakes great enterprises, not on account of the rich but on account of virtue.

Again, no part of the State is to be organised in such a way that it seems to be completely self-contained, but it is to be organised so that it contributes to all the parts and so that it works for the common welfare of the whole State. If it were otherwise, neither the State itself nor any of its parts could stand.

He further puts a measure on the growth of the State, so that it remains a single State; for at the first sign that the unity is in danger of being lost the State must not be allowed to expand any further. He therefore decrees that the State should be neither tiny nor vast, but middling in size, well-balanced, and harmonious, so that its unity is protected.

But since the man who is careless at seed-time waits in vain for the harvest, Plato thinks that the whole focus of attention should be given to childhood and youth, as if sowing for a refined harvest; so that a careful reckoning is kept of all the words, games, and deeds of the boys and youths. If this stage of life is overlooked, all exertion in relation to everyday laws will be in vain, like the efforts to administer daily doses of drugs to someone who has no desire to observe any measure in moderating his life. At this point, remember that games gradually change into enthusiasms and ways of living.

Again, just as a man who is robust by nature, sensible, and restrained in his ways never needs medicines, so a State which has been really well established from its inception and has continued within that framework has no need of numerous laws at the beginning and no need of incessant decrees thereafter. But bad States busy themselves in their daily administration with the promulgation of new laws and never prosper. This is why Plato gives no heed to laws in this best of States, for he trusts that the level-headed good men will be the living laws.

But what of the sacred laws? He thinks that even less effort is called for here. For no one will ever understand why God should be worshipped until he has first understood God. But we cannot see the divine Sun unless the divine Sun reveals itself. He therefore thinks that the laws of religion should be sought from Apollo, that is, from the divine light, and that they should be requested not with the tongue but with a mind purified and calm.

I leave out at this point the account of the oracles, for it is very well known. But the allegorical meaning is that Apollo, the divine light, is seated, or firmly present, at the centre of the earth, that is, at the heart of all things everywhere; he rests in the navel, that is, in the mind which is detached from the senses and is turned back to itself in the manner of the shape and movement of a sphere. Apollo, moreover, is like a father to all, being present and intimate and personal: a father to those being born, and finally a fatherland to those returning.

But once the State has been established, Plato recognises four virtues within it. In the guardians there is wisdom, the right knowledge of how to protect and how to take counsel together. In the soldiers there is courage, the firm resolve, despite enticements or threats, to be bold in defending their country when in danger, as far as the laws and the magistrates will determine.

Temperance resides in the leaders, the soldiers, and the craftsmen alike: a common purpose to which all willingly subscribe and by which some give orders and others obey; and among those who obey there are some who obey in warfare and others who obey in the workplaces. This common purpose is not obstructed by any pleasures, for the desires of those who are lower are moderated by the decree and counsel of those who are higher.

Justice, too, is within all, and by justice everyone fulfils his own work and function – the work for which he is best equipped by nature and enthusiasm – both publicly and privately, for the sake of the common good, and no one arrogates another's function to himself.

But when he calls temperance the harmony of the Diapason, understand him to mean the consonance of the Diapason which arises from the double ratio of tension, speed, and force in relation to that which is twice as relaxed, twice as slow, and twice as gentle. From this double ratio there arises the space between the high note, or eighth note, and the low note. And this is as it should be, because the first ratio is that of the double between two and one, and in this first ratio the number two, while seeming to exceed one, creates one anew and doubles it. Then, as two moves and turns upon itself, it produces eight, the three-dimensional number: for two times two times two makes eight.

Now this is called the Diapason, 'through all'; for such a harmony holds all within itself and is reproduced within all. And Plato's words are not wide of the mark when he says that temperance, like the Diapason, includes the highest citizens as well as the lowest and the intermediate ones. For the octave contains the low note, the highest note, and the intermediate notes. But to return to justice: just as, within the harmony of the Diapason, the eighth note is in harmony with the low note, being its double, so, within a well-ordered State, the authority of temperance harmonises so fittingly with the strength of justice that these two virtues can hardly be distinguished one from the other.

And see how appropriately Socrates moves from the Diapason harmony of the eighth note to justice, which the followers of Pythagoras relate to the number eight. For since justice is a totally equitable arrangement based on the merits of each person and is also the firm foundation of the State, it is right to speak of it in relation to the number eight. For this number is the first of the solids and also the first of all solids to break down into even numbers, that is, into two fours, so that this very quotient is likewise resolved equally into numbers which are also even, that is, two twos. And the equity which resolves this number is also the equity by which it is built up, for two times two times two gives eight, as we have said, which is the image of just equality.

And so, whenever Orpheus wished to invoke divine justice, he took his oath on eight divinities: Fire, Water, Earth, Sky, Moon, Sun, Light, and Night. Again, it was well known, as Evander testifies, that on the Egyptian column which had been set up in honour of justice the names of eight divinities were incised: Saturn, Rhea, Osiris, Spirit, Sky, Earth, Night, and Day. Finally, the whole of antiquity thought that the pattern of celestial justice was displayed in the eight spheres.

Socrates shows next that injustice brings quick ruin to a State when certain individuals, usurping what belongs to others, throw everything into confusion and chaos. Justice, on the other hand, is the order and protection of the State.

So now he moves from the more obvious justice of the State to the less obvious justice which lies hidden, as it were, in the soul, and he divides the powers of the soul into three: reason, which represents the guardian; wrath, which stands for the soldier; and appetite, which reflects the craftsman. And he shows that within us there is a single soul in which those three powers naturally reside, distinct each from the others not according to position but according to quality. This refutes some of the loud-mouthed followers of Aristotle and may become clear to anyone who reads attentively. But he makes this distinction in order to show the close similarity between the soul and the State and between the justice of the one and the justice of the other. This is why he says that since the soul is unable, through a single power, to perform opposite actions simultaneously in relation to the same thing, it is necessary for the soul to have at least three powers. For indeed the soul may be drawn towards pleasure by appetite and simultaneously restrained by reason. It may shrink from battle on account of appetite and at the same time be spurred to the fight by wrath. From this it is clear that reason is different from appetite, while the force of wrath is also different from appetite and from reason; this is the case both in boys, who do not yet make use of reason but are boiling with wrath, and in others who perform many actions through wrath and in defiance of the law of reason. He shows that the force of wrath is closer to reason because outrage often serves reason in its opposition to appetite.

He then concludes that justice, together with temperance, is a lawful harmony of the three parts which we have mentioned: the parts within each and every soul and the similar parts within a State. This harmony lies in governing, fulfilling, and obeying; and in carrying out one's own duties and not usurping those of another. And it is not without good reason that to justice, the sister of temperance, he gives the name of harmony, which is made up of the high notes, the low notes, and the intermediate notes, which are related to the leaders and the merchants, with the soldiers coming between them.

Then in order to give an answer to the question that was put a long time ago as to what justice and injustice beget within the soul, he says that virtue is the health, beauty, and strength of the soul, whereas vice is disease, ugliness, and weakness; for virtue orders and protects all the parts of the soul as nature decrees, while vice, on the other hand, throws the order of nature into confusion and chaos. But since it is better to die than to live when the nature of the body has been completely deformed, even if we are supplied with an abundance of external things, he concludes that the life of the man in whom the soul, by which we live, has been deformed by vice should be shunned by all as something wretched.

Finally, at the very end of this book, he declares that the soul and the State which he has described are the best and the happiest: I mean the royal soul and the royal State as ordered by the queen, the reasoning power of man. He adds that government of this kind is called royal when one man, among many good men, clearly excels them all, and that the State of noble men, where most people seem to be equally excellent, is to be considered as such a government in all respects. He also indicates that in the next book he will distinguish in their order the four remaining characteristics both of souls and of States.

The Theme of the
Fifth Book of the *Republic*

I AM NOT UNAWARE that there will be some who are looking for an *Apology* from us, a defence of this fifth book, which proposes the common possession of all things within the State, against the false accusations levelled by slanderers as well as by the ignorant. But they should read Plato himself. I beg them to read carefully and to judge without hostility. Then – I know what I am saying – they will require no *Apology*.

Thus, when the Phoebean Plato, physician to the human race, observed that individual people, families, and States were universally suffering from serious chronic illnesses and that, despite all the medicaments of the State physicians who had been treating them in vain for such a long time, they were either not free of their diseases or perhaps there was just a slight alleviation or a slight improvement, he displayed wisdom and piety by having recourse to that law, highly regarded among physicians, by which the medical authorities ordain that if a patient shows no improvement after certain medicines, for example cold medicines, have been administered for a long time, it is right to resort eventually to warm medicines.

Finding, therefore, that the human race, after countless ages, was deriving no benefit from laws which allowed private property and, indeed, was continually getting worse, Plato had recourse, and not without good reason, to the laws of friendship, which decree that all things should be common among friends, so that, with the removal of division and the cause of division and unhappiness, we might attain harmony, unity, and bliss.

But let us make a new start. At the beginning of the fourth book Socrates, putting the training of the youth before all other laws, briefly hinted that this training would be best if wives, children, and property were held in common. But since this idea is strange to most people and unheard of by most, he is summoned right at the beginning of the fifth book to speak of it more fully and to justify it more substantially. Yet now, since you have learnt from *Critias* and *Timaeus* that a similar system had once obtained in the neighbourhood of Greek and Egyptian Athens, you will not be too shocked by it as something outlandish, or hear of it with mistrust as something deeply troublesome, or accept it reluctantly as something that is not good.

I pass over the many reports among the Bohemi that the city of Placa was once governed in a similar fashion. And what is more, Diodorus writes of an island towards the south of the Ocean in which wives, as well as all else, were in common and the people were enthusiastic students of philosophy and astrology. Pomponius Mela, too, is a witness that the Garamans tribe in distant parts of Africa had all things in common in their State.

It has further been verified that there was a similar sharing of property among the Brahmin philosophers, the Gymnosophists, the Essaei, the followers of Pythagoras, and lastly among the saints who established the early Christian Republic. We also see in our own times that those religious people among whom there is no private property attain to virtue and happiness.

But if the concept of wives in common troubles you, at least grant first of all that in Plato's view that which adulterous priests commonly regard as sacrilegious is rightly enacted on the basis of law. Then, before you make a judgement, hear the noble words of Plato himself as he holds forth in support of his own cause.

In what follows note firstly the providence displayed by Socrates in deeming that making an error in the establishment of laws is worse than manslaughter; for such an error, perpetuated for centuries, slays many souls as well as bodies. Then note the restraint, reluctance, and obligation with which difficult matters are tentatively approached. Observe, thirdly, the devotion with which he characteristically invokes divine assistance in serious matters. And to avoid making mistakes when establishing laws, he prays for help from the goddess Adrastea, to whom he has also referred in the *Phaedrus*.

According to the ancient theologians, Adrastea is the all-powerful queen of inexorable laws, such as the Saturnian laws relating to minds and the Jovian laws relating to natures. I call Adrastea divine providence insofar as nothing can escape her eyes or slip through her hands. And it is not beside the point that when he wishes to establish the most steadfast of laws – laws which no forgetfulness can obliterate, no craftiness can deceive, no force can break, and none can avoid in any respect – he beseeches Adrastea, who ratifies the inevitable, that no one will be able to avoid them.

Then he progresses step by step to the general training, moving from the organisation of the men to a similar organisation of the women, ordaining that all pursuits – private and public, for peace and for war – be common for the women and the men alike, so that the human race does not become enfeebled; but with the proviso that in all matters the heavier tasks are to be entrusted to the men and the lighter tasks to the women. In the same way he teaches elsewhere that the two arms should be exercised so that everybody is skilful with both and can be called ambidextrous; he shows that this is both useful and possible and how it can be achieved.

Then he brings in the common sharing of wives and children. And at this point mark the great foresight he displays in the order of priority with which he establishes the magistrates, the custodians of marriages, the sacred ceremonies, and the appointed seasons and ages, always ensuring that nothing is done immoderately or to the detriment of the State.

And after the birth, see how carefully he considers the nurture of the new-born children, but in such a way that the man and the woman do not know their own child, while the children do not know their own parents, but all older people are obliged to consider all younger people as their children or grandchildren, and the younger ones, in their turn, look upon all their elders as their parents and likewise upon people of their own age as their brothers and sisters.

When he gives no heed to the nurture of a child who has been born outside the law, whether it be to a useful person or to a useless person, you should understand that it is not a question of his being killed but of being nurtured more humbly in a somewhat secluded place or on the outskirts of the city, beyond the reach of those very precise regulations which govern the upbringing of those who are deemed suitable to become guardians: he is to be brought up on a lower system of regulation so that in due time he can be sent to attend to the less important duties of town or country; or perhaps he will be moved to another city soon after birth.

You will soon come to appreciate the concept of love in common as he arranges everything in such a way that everyone, when shown the same thing or the same person, will make the same judgement and will say, 'This is mine'. And since all are very fond of what is theirs, they will all take care of everything, especially as they are directed towards such care by the laws and the magistrates. In this way, therefore, our own lack of care, our own negligence, which we show towards all things, as if they were foreign to us, is removed. That perennial illusion is also removed by which our judgement is foolishly deceived into cultivating that which we believe to be our own. In short, there is the removal of that extreme perturbation, anxiety, and wretchedness which oppresses us, coming, as it does, from our delirious love for our own possessions.

I merely touch upon the fact that once the cause of discord has been removed, spiritual love will be universal and perfect. In the same way, mark how economical, just, and gentle the laws of war are which he promulgates, and mark the rewards which await the victors in the form of some kind of divinity; for he says that the victors are changed into the blessed spirits which care for mankind and which are to be duly honoured as beloved gods.

But what is said about boys' kisses is one of Glaucon's jests and was spoken merely to relieve the feeling of heaviness. There is also a note of triumph and celebration.

It remains to be shown that it is possible to achieve this common possession, once its excellence has been declared. Firstly therefore he shows that, even if it cannot be achieved, he has not introduced the subject to no avail, for it is the model to be followed as far as possible in the formation of a State. He then shows that it can be achieved only when philosophers rule and that until that time there will be no respite from evils.

This is why he rightly moves on to the subject of shaping philosophers as future helmsmen of State, teaching us the nature of the ability, the disposition, and the training of a State Philosopher. Firstly, just as the people are eager and curious to perceive these lower objects of the senses, so the mind of the philosopher is equally inclined and keen to discover the ideal principles of all these things and is a shrewd hunter of truth itself.

But since real things are Ideas, while natural things are the forms and images of Ideas, it is not without good reason that he says that the people are dreaming, for they think that images are real things. The philosopher, alone of all men, is awake. And since Plato posits a mean between being and non-being, remember that all things are to be considered in five levels. Pure non-being is described as something that is imagined to be beneath matter; but pure being, pure mind, and pure Idea exist. Soul and heaven are said to be both being and non-being, whereas matter has more non-being than being, and the things compounded by nature beneath the Moon are equally being and non-being.

Knowledge focuses on those things which truly are, while ignorance deals with those things which truly are not, and opinion turns about those things which equally are and are not. He ascribes ignorance and opinion to both the people and the Sophists, but he attributes understanding or knowledge to the philosophers alone.

Now when he calls knowledge and opinion a certain power, you should understand him to mean a power that is not without form, for it is endowed partly with natural form and partly with constitution. Moreover, when he treats of Ideas, to which the knowledge of the philosopher is related, he characteristically speaks of the Good, the Beautiful, and the Just. The number three is here expounded in three ways. According to the first way, the Good is God; the Beautiful is the multi-faceted angelic mind; and the Just is the celestial soul which apportions the things of the world in an equitable manner. According to the second way, the Good is the very form and act of the divine nature; the Beautiful is the intelligence of the divine nature; and the Just is the will of the divine nature. According to the third way, the Good, among Ideas, is the model of every form, act, and nature; the Beautiful is the model of the order which arises from every form and resonates within it; and the Just is the model of the order which every form and thing relate to other forms.

But when he substitutes the evil for the Good, the foul for the Beautiful, and the unjust for the Just, take care to put these three as opposites within Ideas. Put them with the formlessness and deformity of matter, which in the book *On Knowledge* he calls the model that is devoid of divinity, and which in the *Statesman* he calls the place of dissimilarity; and put them in that soul, too, which is already deformed and completely turned towards matter.

Finally, because the riddle of the eunuch touches upon something childish, here it is: 'A man who was not a man, seeing but not seeing, struck but did not strike, with a stone that was not a stone, a bird that was not a bird above a tree that was not a tree.' The meaning is that a one-eyed eunuch struck with a pomegranate the wing of a bat above an elder-tree. But I know you will laugh at this, and it is a fitting means of arousing laughter.

The Theme of the
Sixth Book of the *Republic*

AS ALL LAWS, even the best, are lifeless in the absence of truly upright magistrates, while the best magistrates, even without written laws, are themselves living laws, our Plato is right, as we have explained elsewhere, to take every care to train magistrates rather than to establish laws in his excellent State; and he takes great pains to do so not only from very early childhood but even from the time of conception, so that from selected seed and continuous nurture the best fruit might be obtained.

But since he calls them guardians, and since it is very fitting for guardians to look to the future and to reflect, he selects for the task of guarding the human flock a temperament that is particularly philosophic and indubitably more clear-sighted than all others. Indeed, since it is only to the eyes of such a man that there is revealed that model of the Good itself and of justice in whose image the State may well be depicted with justice and happiness, it also behoves the guardian to be truthful, noble, restrained, courageous, just, magnanimous, and gentle.

Plato will demonstrate that these are also the qualities of the philosopher, so that he concludes, in brief, that the function of guardianship should be entrusted to the philosopher before all others. This is why he will first of all show that this is the nature of the philosopher; and then, because a noble nature that has not been properly nurtured is always useless and very frequently harmful, he will transmit the training needed to cultivate such a temperament.

But prior to that he treats of the false and counterfeit philosopher who imitates the true philosopher; of the misuse of philosophy; and of the practice of philosophy which is eminently right for the man who will one day rule the State.

Now he teaches that what is most fitting for a philosopher is constant love for truth itself in relation to matters eternal; and that for this reason falsehood and love of the temporal are more remote from the philosopher than anything else is. He further shows that the mind of the philosopher, in its search for truth, is separated from the body; that, through some affinity of its own, it is united with the divine mind; and that, through the patterns of Ideas implanted within it from the beginning, it attains the Ideas themselves and from its contact with them it sheds light, so that it soon becomes more fertile in conceiving the truth and stronger in giving birth to the truth: in other words, through its conceptions it harmonises with Ideas in all places. But take note at this point that the act of understanding is called begetting and giving birth, as it is in the *Symposium*. This concurs with Christian theology and shows that within the mind are truth and a form which is natural as well as composed of images.

In the same way he thinks that such a temperament is very rare and is innate in very few people, and even in those cases it is in need of many qualifications and is hampered by many obstacles. In particular, he thinks that it is distorted by what the crowd says and believes, and even more by what it does, as well as by riff-raff instructors who adapt their own life and speech to the mob in fawning adulation and pass a similar way of life on to their hearers. And see how apt Plato is in comparing the mob to a great brute and in comparing all States to ships which are ruled by sailors who are totally ignorant of seamanship and who laugh at a man who is accomplished in seafaring.

Take note that any gifts of nature or fortune turn bad if neglected, and become totally worthless if badly tended. Note further that if occasionally, although very rarely, some great and absolutely upright man appears in a State that is badly organised, as Plato judges them all to be, this is ascribed to nothing less than divinity rather than to art or nature.

But when he speaks of Momus, the god of censure, you should understand that Momus is the divine care which foresees what might have been censured in events if they had been different from what they are, and which therefore arranges all events so that they cannot be justifiably censured.

He accordingly gives the reasons why slanders have been cast against the philosophers, with allegations that they are either evil or useless to the State. Firstly, many who are quite unsuited to the pursuit of philosophy on account of their distorted temperament and their paucity of judgement – though they have no shortage of ambition or greed – encroach upon philosophy and seize hold of her, and from their contact with her they generate opinions which are spurious and derisory. They dishonour the practice of philosophy with their ways. Secondly, any who are born to study philosophy are quickly misled by unsound training and practices; or, if they manage to keep their character intact, are not given suitable levels of training; or, when they are trained, are not admitted to the State, or, rather, they themselves have no wish to plunge into the sea of public affairs, fearing inevitable dangers and having no hope that they will be able to benefit the State with sound advice when surrounded by corrupt men.

Among other topics, notice the storms of the active life, the calmness of the contemplative life, the exalted mind of the philosopher, his contempt of all that is mortal, his pursuit of what is divine, and a system for giving instruction according to the different stages of life. He instructs the philosopher and the citizen on exactly identical principles, and there is no harm in this; for he declares in the *Statesman* and the *Sophist* that the princely man, the civilian, and the philosopher are one and the same person.

But he shows that two qualities which very seldom occur together in human beings need to co-exist in the same man: a nature that is keen-witted, good at contemplation, and burning with eagerness for the truth, and a nature that is serious, vigorous in action, and able to make provision for the public welfare. A man with such a disposition will endure through all the steps of training, as will be made clear in the seventh book. Plato also orders him to be practised in all the activities of city life and to be thoroughly tried and tested, as gold is by fire, in the midst of pleasures, sorrows, toils, and dangers, before the helm of State is entrusted to him.

But Plato judges that first and foremost this man needs the knowledge of the Good itself, which is the most important knowledge of all, and he states that just as the possession of anything without the possession of the Good is useless, so the knowledge of all things and of all arts is totally useless without the understanding of the Good itself, and that no citizen can properly direct anything, private or public, towards the Good unless he knows, through reason, what the Good is.

Although the knowledge of this divine Good may seem to a follower of Aristotle to be unnecessary for men's characters in governing a State, it is in fact necessary for the very act of governing, by means of which, as Plato says earlier, efforts should be made to render the citizens and their friends like unto God. He further adds that, in relation to the need to organise all good things by reference to the Good itself, the helmsman is blind and is led to do this fortuitously unless he has discerned the primal form of the Good, the model and cause of all that is good.

But in order to be aware that Aristotle in his *Ethics* is jesting with the Idea of the Good in opposition to Plato, you should read Plato's words with the utmost care, and then you will clearly see that the Idea of the Good is not this or that type, is not here or there, but is the abundance of the highest Divinity, pervading all things with its power, its sweetness, and its wholesomeness.

He says that its image in the visible world is the visible Sun, which likewise diffuses its powers through all things. But Plato thinks that, prior to this Sun which we see, there is another Sun, the primal image of God the Father: the true Son. He speaks of the sons of the Good in order that you may contemplate, above this visible son with the nature of an image, the invisible archetype.

We read of this Father and Son in Plato's letter to Hermias; and Philo, a follower of Plato, speaks of this in his book on *Causes* when he says:

'The effort should be made principally to rise up to being itself, of which it is said, "I AM THAT I AM", or at least to its image and most sacred principle, the first-born Word.'

Through this principle and word all things are made, according to Heraclitus and Plato. Amelius, another follower of Plato, declares the same and bases his words on the testimony of St John the Evangelist. Plato makes the same solemn declaration in his *Epinomis*. And although some of his followers, particularly Julian in his book *On the Sun*, make a distinction of substance, in the manner of the Arians, between God, the Son of God the Father, and the Father Himself, Julian's teacher, Iamblichus, puts forward the Mysteries of the Egyptians, in which there is one principle for the Father and a different principle for the Son, although the substance seems to be the same.

But hear the Mystery. The first God is also the one Father of the first God, whom He begot whilst remaining in the single unity of Himself. But He is the model of the Son, who is named Son of Himself, Father of Himself, and sole Father, God who is truly good. For He is the source of Ideas, and from this undoubtedly single source the self-sufficient God has unfolded Himself into light. This is why He is called self-sufficient and Father to Himself, for He is the beginning, God of Gods, the One from the One, above all essence, and the beginning of essence. Iamblichus bears witness that this Mystery is of Hermes.

But at this point Plato briefly indicates in what way the Good Itself is above desire and character and wisdom. It is above desire, because if desire itself were the Good Itself no desire would be evil or harmful.

It is above character, because many people think that they have a good character if they appear to have a good character; but because they consider the true to be the Good they do not seek to possess it through opinion but through the thing itself. It is also above knowledge, because you do not desire to know random things or to know them in a random way, but you desire to know good things and to know them well; otherwise you are rejecting knowledge or disregarding it.

Nor should you say that the Good Itself is the knowledge of the Good, for then you would be foolishly defining something by itself. Again, it is above the intellect, for the intellect strives hard to attain the Good, but the Good Itself never seeks the Good. It is also above truth, for the more you judge something to be good the more you choose it; but you prefer disease and deprivation, which are less true, to something that is more true. Finally, it is above being, for in order to be well you need to be. But in the *Theology* we speak more fully of these matters and of how it is by the light of the Good Itself that the intellect perceives all that is true.

Next comes the differentiation of things into two kinds, the visible and the invisible; and each of these is divided into two, the prior and the subsequent; and there is a similar differentiation with human perception. In these matters he follows Brontinus and Archytas, but he expounds such subjects more fully and more felicitously than they do.

The Theme of the
Seventh Book of the *Republic*

THE WISE, being endowed with divine qualities, make every effort to turn the whole focus of their mind from the earthly to the celestial, from the moving to the still, and from what is perceived through the senses to that which transcends the senses. Holding that the organisation of the cosmos is one, that it is marvellously ordered, but that it cannot be made from itself, since it is composed of diverse elements and is subject to change, they are right to recognise that it depends on that, I mean on another One, which abounds in wisdom and which composes a single work from many elements, puts it into wise order universally and rules it with might: this vast complex work, which revolves with a movement that is perpetual and very fast but not erratic. This One also shows the greatest benevolence in guiding all things towards the Good with wonderful appropriateness and smooth ease.

This is why they all agreed, through a common conception, that God is the one King of creation – powerful, wise, and merciful – whom earthly kings and rulers of State should strive to imitate. After this common conception of God they began to set out, quite openly and quite close together, along twin pathways to God: the pathway of negating and the pathway of relating. For by the first pathway they discussed what the Good Itself, by which they meant God, is not, and thus they showed that it is nothing that is perceived through the senses and nothing that is understood by the mind. By the second pathway, however, they related creatures to a Creator and, conversely, a Creator to creatures; and they pondered on how a Creator might make and perfect all things and how creatures might be related to the Creator or be able to imitate or attain the Creator.

In *Parmenides* Plato shows what he confirms in Book Six, namely, that the mind of the student of philosophy proceeds thus far, and Dionysius the Areopagite, too, gives this his fullest approval: proceeds thus far, I say, by a ray of light imparted just once to the mind at the beginning and by the approaching light which constantly illumines minds with divine blessings. But, as Plato shows both in *Parmenides* and here, no one can understand through such pathways what the Good in itself actually is: the divine substance. Along these pathways one can merely reach the point at which the divine Good, through its kindly grace alone, shapes with its own radiance its ever-approaching lover, cherishes him with its warmth, and through its power transforms his mind, which finally knows God once it has become God. This is what Plato also indicates in his letters.

But only after the philosopher has contemplated God, who rules the heavens, will he, and he alone, be able to rule the earth in god-like fashion. On this subject Plato praises Minos, who sought laws from Jupiter through contemplation before proclaiming them to the people. I merely mention the great praise that many bestow on Scipio because he came before the State with Jupiter as his teacher. What shall I say of Numa Pompilius, who governed the State with religious laws? And did not the Mosaic laws, by which the people of God were divinely governed, reach men through the instruction of God Himself? This is why Aristoxenus gives an account of the mysteries of the Hindu philosophers, which record that without divine rule, a rule revealed by God, nothing private or public can ever be rightly and happily administered.

But since this is what the Egyptians found, they entrusted the helm of rule to philosophers alone, indeed to master philosophers who were also holy men. And they were so convinced that nothing could be happily managed without divine help that they inaugurated all public undertakings with rites and prayers. As Iamblichus reports, their assertion that nothing could be understood without divine inspiration was so strongly held that all their philosophical books were attributed to the name of the god Hermes, as if they were the works of God rather than of men. This is what *Timaeus* means when it says that philosophy is a divine gift. In *Protagoras* and the *Statesman* Plato also teaches that experience in civic affairs is a divine gift.

But let us return to the seventh book. Plato does not allow anyone to govern his State except the man known to have received both of these gifts through some divine quality and divine training, the man whom he always calls the rightful citizen and philosopher. But why does he say that a divine gift is essential for this? Leaving other reasons aside for the moment, I say that since it is very difficult for anyone to govern himself happily, it is certainly impossible without God, the author of happiness, ever to provide a happy organisation for a State, which is made up of so many diverse elements and which is daily at the mercy of so many mishaps.

Hence it has come about that all States have acknowledged a deity of their own as their protector or patron. Plato sees the representative and interpreter of this deity as the ruler of the State, who, acting for the deity, contemplates the divine and thus provides for the human. For this reason he drives far away from the State all bad men, who seem to be completely devoid of the divine gift. He accepts good men only; yet not all good men, for those who are ignorant of theology he calls blind dreamers, similar to those who take the images of things for the things themselves, and he considers it foolish to entrust the protection of the State to blind dreamers. But even theologians who have as yet no practical experience of human affairs he does not allow to manage public matters until he has first made them accustomed to dealing with private and less serious concerns. He here concludes that the magistracy should be given to no one whose life does not excel the magistracy and who neither seeks nor even desires the magistracy.

Now when Plato, in training the civic philosopher, puts forward the image of the cave, the chains, the light, the shadows, and the water, you should understand that the cave is this visible world when compared to the invisible world; the chains symbolise the human body, or rather the agitation which binds the soul to the body; the shadows are all those things which activate the senses, for such things are the shadows of the real things, the Ideas. His statement that the soul cannot quickly move down from the invisible world to the visible world, or rise up again, without suffering pain can be understood in two ways, according to the Platonic tradition: firstly, in this life, when a move is made, without intermediary, from the usual pursuit of what is human to the highest pursuit of what is divine, and also when the reverse move is made; and secondly, when the move is made between this life and the next, that is, when the soul, even if impure, moves from the shadow of the body to the divine light, where it is quite dazzled and tormented, or when the soul, coming down from the divine light into a body composed of elements, is blind and troubled for a long time.

But remember that it is the property of light to make and reveal everything, and remember that light is threefold: divine, intellectual, and visible. The divine light is called the Sun of the other two Suns; the intellectual light is called the angelic Sun, the Sun of the universal Sun; and lastly, the visible light is the Sun in the heavens and its effulgence. But just as the effulgence from the celestial Sun, being diffused throughout all things, is the image and activity of the Sun, so the light which is within the Sun is the image and activity of the angelic mind. Then the light within the angelic mind is the activity and image of the divine light. And just as visible light is received only in a transparent nature, so invisible light is received in a perspicacious nature.

Julian the Platonist, writing of these three Suns in his book *On the Sun*, adds, from the theology of the Phoenicians, that visible light is a continuous activity of the divine and angelic intelligence flashing out to the eyes through the solar aperture and being diffused thence through transparent materials everywhere, which seem to be compatible with it. However that may be, have no doubt that that light is not a body, for it penetrates bodies without imparting hurt or stain; and it does not become a specific quality of the compound body, for, if it were to, it would need its own warm or cold quality from the elements, a quality prior to it which it would assume, and when the Sun in due time receded, the light would remain in the transparent body. Again, it is not confined to a specific measure, for it does not arrive at a particular time or illumine one part now and another part later.

Furthermore, light can fill a vast space without being dissipated and, on the other hand, it can enter a confined space in an instant without harming itself or the container. And it is not in fact corporeal, but it is the medium between the incorporeal and the corporeal and it is undoubtedly the special quality of the heavens, whose nature is as close to the incorporeal as it is possible to be.

Light is also transmitted to the elements provided that they are transparent, and it is their very transparency which makes them like unto the heavens. To what is transparent, light is transmitted first, and then heat; to what is opaque, heat is transmitted first, but light is not transmitted until what is opaque is restored to a transparent state through the operation of heat. Light, however, does not pour into opaque bodies in which an earthy condition predominates: not because it is unable to penetrate them, since it can penetrate glass, which is denser than many opaque bodies, but because the earthy condition, which is quite alien to the nature of the heavens, cannot contain its heavenly quality. Yet it does transmit heat to opaque bodies, as I have said, since heat is not so fully a property of the heavens as light is. For it is because they shine that the heavens give heat.

But the light which is diffused by the heavens upon the transparent bodies of our world should be called the image of the Sun. This is clear from the fact that it is the general and the specific origin of all images. For images of things arise from the radiance of this light, and this light is such a potent image that it is manifest not only when it rebounds from a reflective body but also when it springs forth from the Sun, because it is not compatible with any other images. However, they are all incorporeal, since they pervade everything in an instant, and there can be many at the same point without any disorder.

Thus light is incorporeal, and its nature is perfected by its power. Remember that in the same way a ray of the Sun carries with it the activity of radiance and the force of heat; through radiance, brightness is given back to the divine and angelic intelligence, while through heat are conveyed both the disposition of will and the love which pertain to the divine and angelic intelligence. But since the powers above, like craftsmen, carry out their work through will rather than through intelligence, it is right for this visible ray, which flows forth from their invisible ray, to act through heat, rather than through radiance, in producing all that is produced. But, of course, it does act through radiance to produce the airy images of things, and through heat to produce physical qualities. And so this heat depends on radiance, just as all things are ideally portrayed through the intellect, whereas it is through the disposition arising therefrom that all things are begotten.

Let us then heed the warning that the earthly nature is not receptive to celestial light and let us drive far from us all earthly tendencies, so that we may be filled with divine light. And if the last body does not accept the light of the first, unless it is warmed and made similar to it, there is nothing for it but to burn with the love of the last mind before burning with the love of the first mind, so that, being purified by love and being made similar, we may then shine like deities and rejoice in the fullness of light.

But let us touch on the remaining points in the seventh book. Since, as we have said, light is thus threefold – visible; intellectual and transcending sight; divine and transcending the intellect – Plato here speaks of light at three levels: light in the cave, light by night, and light by day. He also makes a threefold reference to water – water in the cave, water at night, and water by day – for just as light makes and reveals all things, so water washes and reflects all things. By means of the first Plato signifies character, and by means of the second he indicates contemplation. And he traces both of them through three levels.

Of course, through moral training there is a threefold process of washing and purification: firstly, pruning the less important activities by means of the civil virtues; secondly, rooting them out by means of the purifying virtues; and thirdly, fully tempering the important activities through the virtues of the newly purified mind.

From here the move is made, particularly through contemplation, to the model virtues which are in God. There are also three levels of contemplation, which the water that is mentioned three times symbolises, insofar as it denotes intelligence by reflecting the images. For things divine seem, as I have said, to be reflected in three waters. They are firstly reflected indistinctly in physical laws, then more clearly in mathematical laws, and thirdly, with total clarity, in the perfect principles of metaphysics.

Plato says that physical forms are material through and through, because they require both general and specific matter and they cannot be conceived without it, while mathematical forms are less material because they do not require specific matter: they require general matter, as is the case with measurements, or none at all, as is the case with numbers; and it is permissible to conceive of them without matter. Finally, he considers divine forms as completely immaterial and as true things whose images are the mathematical forms and whose shadows are natural things. This is a Pythagorean mystery.

And so, when he observes that Thales, Democritus, and Anaxagoras were as careless in divine matters as they were careful in natural matters, whereas Pherecydes and Pythagoras, as well as the followers of Pythagoras, were all leading mathematicians and, at the same time, the greatest theologians, conducting themselves like gods, he rightly came to the conclusion, partly through reason and partly through experience, that the painstaking pursuit of natural forms is very frequently responsible for turning the mind away from the divine.

This is why Solomon judged this to be the worst of occupations, and those who are excessively immersed in it to be wretched. In the *Phaedo* Socrates calls down a curse upon such men, who, I say, go to a great deal of trouble to relate the causes of natural effects purely to some elemental qualities and thus come to a halt in such a beginning and such an end, failing to search out the supreme beginning and the supreme end of the universe.

For this reason, when the seventh book guides the soul to the highest Good and to the Sun, that is, to God, and to the divine Ideas, which are like stars, and does all this in convenient steps, it makes no mention of natural skill during the ascent itself; but it concentrates on certain mathematical steps which lead without any difficulty towards the divine world. Two of these steps are pure, for arithmetic deals with pure numbers, and geometry with pure measurements. But three of the steps are mixed, for to the numbers music adds notes and movements which pertain particularly to the realm of hearing, while stereometry adds weights to the measurements, and astronomy measures the celestial spheres and their movements with numbers and dimensions.

However, Plato makes use of natural skill in the descent rather than in the ascent, and this is what he frequently teaches in the *Timaeus*, the *Philebus*, and *Parmenides*, and in other places, too. For it is in the descent through the divine causes of the natural world that he wishes natural principles to be demonstrated; but he thinks that in the ascent the anxious care for what is natural, a care that is far removed from things divine, turns the soul away from them rather than towards them.

Now he attributes no value at all to any actions – even if they seem to be most honourable – unless they lead to the imitation and attainment of the divine Good. He likewise gives no heed to any reflections unless they are propitious for discovering the divine Good, and he even rejects them if there is any possibility that they will turn us away from it.

And so he sees the entire study of philosophy as a movement from the perceptible to the intelligible and an ascent to the Good Itself, which is the supreme light of the intelligible realm. He says that just as sight is related to the highest of all that is visible, that is, to the Sun, so the intellect is related to the supreme light of all that is intelligible, that is, to God. Thus, just as the Sun begets the eye and in the process of begetting bestows the power to see and continually makes the activity of seeing available to what has been begotten, so God creates the intellect and in the process of creating bestows the power to understand and continually makes the activity of understanding available to what has been created.

Again, just as in relation to the eye no skill is needed except that of keeping it clean and turning it, so in relation to the intellect philosophy provides two things only, by cleansing it of disturbances and of false opinions and by turning it, through principles and exhortations, away from perceptible forms and towards the intellectual forms which are implanted within us; next, by means of these intellectual forms, towards the intelligible forms, the Ideas; and then, by means of Ideas, towards the divine mind by which the Ideas are embraced; and finally, from the divine mind to the divine Good, the principle and the light of Ideas.

Thus, when he says that the soul is raised from the lamp to the Moon, and from the Moon to the Sun, he means that it is raised from the natural forms to the mathematical forms, and finally from the mathematical forms to the divine forms, not by a process of teaching – for, as he tells us in his letters, divine matters cannot be taught – but by a process of cleansing and turning. For once this process is completed, then just as the Sun, which is the light of all that is visible, reveals to the eye all that is visible, so the Good itself, which is the light of all that is intelligible, reveals to the understanding all that may be understood. But there is much more on these matters in our *Theology*. And so no one should be surprised that Plato seldom makes use of the didactic method of writing, but always employs a method that is purifying and exhortatory, that is, one which has the power to re-direct the soul.

Note next that of all perceptible things those have the greatest power to awaken the intelligence which are not clearly distinguished from their opposites by means of the senses, and for this reason they require a discriminating intelligence. He says further that numbers are not corporeal, since number is nothing other than unity repeated. But unity is not a body, for it cannot be divided into parts, or if one can imagine it being divided, it is not cut but rather multiplied; multiplied, I say, into itself and not into any parts, for every part is considered to be less than the whole. But there is no unity that is greater or smaller than unity. And what is more, this unity and number are able to raise us up to incorporeal essence; and the same power resides in figures, whose true ratio is found in the mind rather than in the body.

Astronomy, likewise, seems to search for the principle of a mover in the order of the heavens. Plato says that the astronomer who has not looked up from the heavens themselves to what is above the heavens does not look upon things eternal, especially since the heavenly bodies do not make a complete system and thus undoubtedly depend on a system that is higher and complete.

He also laughs at the musician who does not move from the harmony of sound to the intellectual principle of harmony.

Finally, he puts dialectic, that is, metaphysics or theology, before all other studies, as their leader, the one who employs the service of each of the others for her own work. Now her work is to go forward throughout the whole extent of what he calls being; to have recourse to the Good Itself, the cause of being in its entirety; and, within the range of beings, to define what each one is by identifying the principle of every essence, or to reveal that which follows every essence. But by the standard of her nobility he deems all other studies to be in bondage. For either they submit to the opinions of men, to the productions and compositions of inferior beings, or to the worship of those things which are begotten; or else they at least strive to raise themselves towards the incorporeal, although to some extent they merely dream about them. Such, he says, are the mathematical disciplines.

But soon he adds two further classes: essence and becoming. He says that intelligence belongs to essence, while opinion belongs to becoming. He then says that, within intelligence, knowledge which belongs to the dialectician attains essence, while notions follow essence and belong to the mathematician. He likewise counts faith and imagination as being within opinion: through faith physical bodies are perceived, while through imagination are perceived the images and shadows of these bodies.

Then he concludes that all other studies, without dialectic, are blind and that they, together with dialectic, are vain if they do not know clearly the Idea of the Good and through this Idea are able to distinguish what is true and good from what is false. The man who does not know the principle of the Good is troubled and deceived by dreams in this life and is even more subject to deceit and harassment when he goes down to the world below.

He adds that that man is lame who has no aptitude for, and no experience of, both action and contemplation. This is why he chooses as helmsmen those who are equipped by nature and adequately trained by discipline for both of these activities. Note at this point that the untruthful man is excluded from the State as if he were crippled and mutilated. The untruthful man he identifies as the man who carefully and deliberately tells lies to others and who, through ignorance, tells lies to himself. Remember that the toils of the mind are more onerous than the toils of the body, and for this reason this should be learnt in youth, and when the liberal arts are taught all servitude should be kept at bay.

Dialectic, however, should not be communicated to young people, as the *Philebus* also teaches us. For, as the *Phaedrus* makes clear, there are two guides within each of us: the innate desire for pleasures and the body of opinion which has been acquired through our education and which directs us, in all matters, to follow what the laws define as honourable and just. But these two guides very frequently pull in opposite directions. Yet since skill in discussion, if communicated to the youths, undermines the view of what is honourable and produces men who are intemperate and even overbearing or irreligious, as we read in the *Philebus* and the *Laws*, instruction in mathematics and practice in public business should be given, at regular intervals, until the thirtieth year of life.

But when they reach their thirtieth year they should be introduced to dialectic, while still being called back from time to time to deal with matters of public interest. Now the art of discussion you should call dialectic from its form, logic from its origin, and metaphysics and theology from its end; and you should know that it is to the virtually divine end of such dialectic that men are summoned in their fiftieth year of life because a purified and calm mind is a prerequisite for insight into the divine.

At this point take note that, both here and in the *Theology*, we quite often refer to the fact that three things are heeded by Plato: the ray, the light, and the radiance. The ray is inherent within individual minds, just as it is a natural property of the eyes. The light is common to all eyes. The divine radiance excels the light which is common to all minds, just as the radiance within the Sun excels the light that is uniformly common to the eyes.

His conclusion is that after a citizen, by means of the ray naturally inherent within him and the light with which he is infused, has contemplated the radiance of the Good Itself, his duty is to use all his powers to govern the State on the model of the Good Itself.

The Theme of the Eighth Book of the *Republic*

SOCRATES HAS NOW presented the perfect form of the State in seven books, a form made sacred by the number seven, which pertains to Pallas Athene. He calls this form the royal government; and he also calls it government by the best, because within this State many outstandingly good men fulfil public functions and constitute the Senate. He calls it royal because all have a single will directed towards the public good and a single mind as their queen; and if any one of them is of exceptional integrity he is accorded exceptional honour. Yet he is not accorded so much honour that he has the power to modify public affairs without the approval of the Senate, which comprises all the upright citizens.

After the best and blessed form of the State, there remains the question of introducing the lesser forms, which he counts as four. He presents the first of these as that into which the best form quickly degenerates, and he calls this 'glory-seeking'. The second form is the power of the few which arises from the glory-seeking State. The third is popular government, which develops from the second form. Lastly, there is the fourth form, the tyranny to which government by the people is particularly prone.

But since the forms of the State arise from the forms of souls, he goes on to describe, with astonishing skill, the five dispositions and ingrained habits of souls which match the States in number and are given similar names. His conclusion, in brief, is that the kingly soul is best and happiest, and the same is true of the State. The tyrannical soul, on the other hand, is the worst and the most wretched, and States which are oppressed by tyrants are likewise the worst and the most wretched. He concludes that the intermediate souls and the intermediate forms of government come between these two extremes.

What becomes clear from all this is, on the one hand, the destructive nature of injustice, both in the State and in the soul, and, on the other hand, the saving grace of justice within both. At all times he explains, with astonishing care, how souls and States change from one form to another. In particular, he shows how the blessed and, so to speak, golden State changes from a lofty starting-point into the glory-seeking or silver State or into the iron State, and he portrays the Muses pouring this forth, or rather blending it together, as an oracle.

Indeed, if the happy State is unable to decline into a worse one through some fault in itself, and yet somehow it does fall eventually, it must decline on account of some general defect and cause. In this matter it is permissible to laugh at the unfounded claims made by Aristotle; for in the fifth book of his *Politics* Aristotle should not have demanded of his Plato – who is never his, in fact – an inherent cause for the change of a happy State, since there is no such cause, but he should have been satisfied with a general cause. For it is in this way that the man who is most robust and most temperate, just like the State in a similar condition, is distressed by a cause that is not so much individual as general, that is, by some sequence which is ordained by fate and which revolves perpetually through the celestial circuits which are beneath the Moon, so that those things which are compounded by particular configurations of the spheres and by particular movements of the ages are at some point dissolved by contrary configurations and movements. But since the attribution of such a cause far exceeds the bounds of the current capability of society, Socrates employs the prophetic power of the Muses, and indeed he employs it in such a way that we, too, have need of the prophetic powers of Apollo to interpret these things.

It is not without some justification that Cicero, when wishing to give a brief explanation of a very abstruse point, says that it is more recondite than Plato's number. And I am not surprised that Theo of Smyrna, that eminent teacher of Platonic mathematics, astutely avoided this mystery as something inexplicable. When Iamblichus of Chalcis tried to unravel it, he seems to have made it more of a tangle. But what if there is more difficulty than weight in such words? Especially since Plato himself portrays the Muses as using the bombast of tragedy to impose upon and terrify the simple mind of the youth and put it into a state of stupor. In short, take whatever may be helpful from our commentaries to the *Timaeus*.

In the meantime ponder the following moral precepts. In a State it is impossible to give honour simultaneously to wealth and to virtue. Handing the helm of State to the wealthy is just like putting a ship into the hands of someone who is well-to-do but has no experience of sailing: both will be put into jeopardy. The surest protection against all forms of vice is knowledge. One of a pair of opposites, taken to extremes, is the beginning of the other one: thus liberty, taken to the extreme of licence, is the beginning of the extreme of servitude, just as, with any quality, an excess of materials or occasions frequently becomes its exact opposite. In his letters Plato says the same, giving his fullest approval to liberty which is moderate.

The Theme of the
Ninth Book of the *Republic*

SOCRATES HAS DEALT at length with the royal life lived by the best men; and he has a long discussion about its opposite, which is tyranny. We consequently approve of the former as the height of happiness and condemn the latter as the depth of wretchedness. Tyranny is discussed not only in the eighth book but in the ninth book as well, principally because it arises, such as it is, from government by the people, as something harmful and unpropitious. We should therefore strive with every sinew to ward off the initial tyranny, which is the tyranny within the soul, and embrace instead the kingdom which is in the depths of the soul. In this way there will be an immediate return to the first theme of the general discussion.

This is undoubtedly how he has decided to show not only that justice merits praise according to the measure of man's opinion but also that justice, through its own nature of wonderful integrity and beneficence, is worthy of the highest respect; whereas injustice is not only to be seen as defective through dread of the laws or of disgrace but is also to be shunned on account of the poison inherent in its harmful nature. But when he speaks of nature, he is sometimes referring to legal and common justice, which is universal virtue, established under the aegis of the laws, and on other occasions he is referring to private justice, which may be distributive (so that through such justice are distributed honours, rewards, and punishments within the State, while within the soul actions and functions are allotted to the parts of the soul in accordance with the intrinsic worth of its nature) or transformative (so that within the State things are exchanged for other things or for money at equitable and lawful valuations, and within the soul acts of service are similarly exchanged in such a way that, just as reason gives counsel to the lower functions, so the lower powers supply what is necessary according to the dictates of reason).

Take note during this discussion that the tyrannical soul is so disturbed that it may rightly be judged to be ruined by passion, intoxicated, frenzied, and brutal, especially since it is seized, like a wild beast, by those brutal passions whose ferocity others experience at times only when dreaming. Now in the *Theology* we deal at length with those things which are related to the falsity, the truthfulness, and the prophetic nature of dreams.

Consider the care with which he enumerates all the evils which oppress a State that is under the heel of tyranny, and the skill with which he lists the same number, and even more, within the soul of the tyrant, with the result that it is impossible to imagine anything more wretched.

He next divides the whole discussion, which aims at putting the wise and just life ahead of its opposite, into three sections. He intends the first section to be what has been dealt with so far, which is a comparison of a foolish and unjust man to a State which is governed by the absence of wisdom and the absence of justice. In this comparison it is clear that such a State and such a man, are, for similar reasons, in desperately wretched straits.

He now begins the second section, repeating the differentiation of the parts of the soul into the reasoning nature, the wrathful nature, and the appetitive nature. To these natures correspond three lives: the philosophic life, the glory-seeking life, and the life of desire. This life of desire for possessions and pleasures is also called the avaricious life. He likewise divides the State into three: the magistrates, the militia, and the traders. He then shows that a life endowed with virtue is to be chosen in preference to a life of vice, and that it is actually more agreeable.

Of course, since each of those three parts puts the pleasure of its own life before that of all the others, only the philosopher is rightly able to decide a question like this, for such a judgement requires experience, wisdom, and reason. As far as experience is concerned, the philosopher has put to the test his own desires and those of other people, so that he is easily able to discern which is to be given preference, whereas others have never savoured the joys known to the philosopher and are thus unable to compare their pleasures with the bliss experienced by the philosopher.

It is, moreover, only the philosopher who is effective in the perfect application of wisdom and in the task of attributing causes, the two further operations needed to form sound judgement. Thus, since the philosopher puts the joys of a wise and just life before the attractions of the ostentatious and sensual life, we would do well to follow the view of the true judge by putting a life ruled by virtue before a life ruined by vice.

Finally, the third section takes its rise from the fact that true pleasure can be found only in the wise and just man; but it is clear that in all other men there is pleasure which is deceitful and shadowy. And so it is plainly shown that pleasures, even the most powerful ones, do not bring satisfaction. But where fulfilment is given and received more truly and completely, and where the means of fulfilment is purer and more efficacious, there the pleasure is truer, more complete, and more extensive. Therefore, since intellect and the truth which is to be understood have a truer and more complete nature than the senses and what is perceived through the senses, and since truth penetrates the intellect more deeply than it does the senses of perception and operates without any admixture of pain, it follows that the pleasure of the intelligence is truer and more complete.

Somehow something mathematical intervenes at this point, the explanation of which you will encounter more appropriately in the commentaries to the *Timaeus*. In the meantime, give close attention to that depiction of the nature of the soul in which you should understand the nature of avarice in the name of the multi-formed beast, the power of wrath in the form of the lion, and reason in the form of the man. And see how clearly he depicts the life of the glory-seeking, unjust, lustful man, which is indeed nothing but wretched servitude.

In the same place you should also grasp the way of understanding how souls move into beasts, so that they may be said to move into the emotions and propensities of beasts rather than into their bodies. Remember, too, that just as, within the body, clarity of the senses, health, strength, and beauty are good by nature and not through opinion, and their opposites are likewise bad, so, within the soul, prudence, temperance, courage, and justice are naturally good, and their opposites are naturally bad.

Finally, assume that form of the entire life by which you may arrange all the bodily elements so that they harmonise with the consonance of the soul; select individual items conducive to the health of the soul, and shun whatever impairs it; dwell for ever in the citadel of the mind, and do not allow yourself to be cast headlong from it by any allurements or threats.

But since you wish to shape yourself and others in this way, adopt the clear model of this State in heaven: in heaven, I say, which is the order of the heavenly movements; and take all that is divine more deeply into your heart and mind, so that you may mould yourself, your family, and your State on this pattern, in justice, happiness, and prosperity.

The Theme of the
Tenth Book of the *Republic*

UNTIL NOW SOCRATES, that most painstaking teacher of the human race, has urged mankind, through the beauty of justice, to move towards the justice of law, that is, towards universal virtue, and conversely he has, through presenting the loathsomeness of injustice, summoned mankind to shun injustice. From this time onwards, however, he will encourage everyone to come closer to justice on account of its everlasting fruits and rewards, and he will deter everyone from embracing injustice on account of its everlasting harmfulness and punishments; and this is the main function of the tenth book.

But before he undertakes this particular function he employs a sort of prologue in which he painstakingly completes something which he had touched upon in the earlier books and had last mentioned at the end of the ninth book: something essential to the welfare of the State. Indeed, this doctor of ours, this physician of human ills, gives particular care to the treatment of that type of illness which all others treat in an offhand manner or, rather, never treat at all.

But what is worse is that they choose and wholeheartedly embrace, as the healthiest thing of all, poetic imitation, by means of which clever poets give keen expression to disturbed souls and, in so doing, impress those same disturbances firmly and deeply into the souls of listeners and readers. The more praise they receive and the more pleasure they give, the more pernicious are the effects upon everybody.

Now a prologue of this kind is a fitting sequel to the end of the ninth book, where the soul is divided into the reasoning part and into the lower parts which are disturbed by agitations and whose rule, firstly within the soul and then within the State, is called tyrannical. But since poetic imitation arouses these lower parts and nurtures and enlarges them, provoking anger, stimulating lust, releasing laughter, opening the channels for tears and cries of grief, it is seen to undermine the rule of reason and to promote the tyranny of disturbance. This is why Socrates eradicates a plague of this nature, which is pleasant in some respects but full of poison, lest it eradicate us.

But observe the great love with which our Plato cares for the whole human race, investigating and seeking out those dangers which no one else would even suspect. Moreover, while struggling stoutly against his own nature and upbringing, which are poetical, he puts up a valiant fight for the public weal. For this reason no one ought to be surprised that Plato, for the love of truth, does not spare even his Homer, since out of devotion to justice he does not make any allowance for his own propensities.

Now his principal purpose in detracting from Homer is that we may consider that through him, as the chief of imitators, all the others should come under much greater condemnation. And since he says that neither matters divine nor matters human are taught by Homer,

46

you should understand that the praises bestowed upon Homer by Plato in the *Philebus* are derived from common opinion and not from Plato's own view. He shows, however, that the skill of imitating is, as we have said, very dangerous and also servile and utterly base, for those who imitate neither understand nor make the things themselves, but, following the forms of things that are apparent to their senses and snatching at the commonly held views of those things, they speak of images and devote themselves to sense impressions and to agitations, without any recourse to reason. Yet whatever disapproval he gives to the poets when they cause agitation, he gives them the same measure of approval if they stimulate us to virtue and holiness through the honourable praise of heroes and through divine hymns.

But in order to convey how base all imitation is, he divides the classification of the arts into three types: the using art, the making art, and the imitating art. And he says that the art which uses the lyre, that is, music, is higher than the art which makes the lyre, since, through the particular purpose that is prescribed for it, he puts its form before that of craftsmanship. But the making art is superior to that of the painter, who makes a copy of the lyre by the use of colours. Just as he considers the poet to convey the images of things to our ears, so he judges that the painter conveys such images to our eyes.

Now at this point some theological questions concerning Ideas are added, but since we have dealt with them at some length in the *Theology* we shall now touch upon them briefly. Come, you devotee of Plato, rise up above those forms which you perceive in the material world and reach that nature which is the mother of those forms. Although you cannot perceive that nature, realise that it pervades the material world like the spirit of life which is full of seeds and which, by means of these seeds, arranges all things with great artistry. Understand that this nature is within the world, just as you understand the vital power to be within you. Therefore, just as you understand that, within you, the perceptive power surpasses the vital nature, so you should, within the world, bring a similar but very general nature back to the source of perception, as if back to something similar but equally general. Then, within yourself, take the senses back to reason, and reason to intellect; and similarly, within the world, take the nature of perception back to the rational nature, and the rational nature back to the intellectual nature.

Moreover, since you perceive within yourself that the intellect seeks that which is intelligible as something more complete than itself, and that the intellect is shaped by the intelligible as if by something more powerful than itself, you should, in the world as in yourself, put the intelligible nature before the intellectual nature. But the intelligible you should call the same in all respects as being itself. Lastly, above what you have called both intelligible and being you should put the Good Itself. For it is on account of the Good Itself that you wish to be well and that you yearn for the intelligible.

When you have ascended thus far, you will perceive the universe, denoted by the sacred number seven, rising from the lowest matter and passing through perceptible qualities, nature, the senses, reason, the intellect, and the intelligible, towards the Good Itself. Moreover, you will see that the good spirit completed all things with the number six, as if on the sixth day, and that it came to rest within itself at the seventh level, as if on the seventh day.

For the Good Itself is the end of all else. Of the Good Itself, therefore, no extraneous end can exist or be imagined. If all things seek the Good, by which they are perfected, it is right to conclude that all things are made by the Good. Again, if it makes all things by its own intrinsic power, understand that the whole universe is enfolded within it. But since its nature is first and is therefore utterly simple, remember that the forms of all things are within it and that its own form is one, and Plato calls this the Idea of the Good Itself, the Idea in which, according to Timaeus, God, the Maker of the world, rested after He had created the world, for he says that the Maker of the world withdrew into His own contemplation.

In the same way, the Idea of the Good produces Ideas, which are the particular forms of all things, distinct one from another by type, within the intelligible nature, by which universal Being is embraced in some intelligible manner, and all intelligence is embraced by a wonderful level of reason which transcends intelligence. All intellects look up to this intelligible nature and from it they receive the enduring exemplars of Ideas. Rational souls, too, look up to it, and from it they have received their exemplars, albeit changeable to some degree. After these exemplars of the rational souls, and after the power of the senses, the images of Ideas go down to the vital nature, seeds, and, moving through qualities, finally reach matter.

Thus when Plato says that God makes the Ideas within nature, understand him to mean within nature and within the intelligible world, the head of the angelic minds. But when he mentions couch and table, these are examples to help you to understand natural things through man-made objects, so that through couch and table you may understand the man who uses them. Again, the example in art seemed more appropriate to the question being put. But perhaps he thinks that the forms which are needed for the regulations of the arts are not far from the Ideas. And he surely does not consider it strange that man has the forms of the arts through divine inspiration, since the fantasies of the arts are present even in beasts. And if such forms occur in the soul through God's inspiration, let them be said to occur in nature, for they are naturally implanted. If someone seems to have little aptitude with regard to certain skills, the followers of Plato will say that he has been distracted by different things or that he has turned to face the opposite direction.

Mark the words of Plato when he says that God does not merely understand, but wills also, for he means that God conceives by understanding within Himself and, through willing, makes outside Himself. Note also that God has expressed the single Idea of a single natural type through the type alone and within the intelligible world itself, for example, the one ideal humanity of the human race; for if in matter, where there is infinite variety and change, a unity of common nature is preserved in each and every man, even more so within a nature that is simple and stable will a single Idea be sufficient for a natural type. Indeed, those things that are varied and unstable can take their common single nature only from the unity of their higher nature.

Again, if two humanities are posited, how can they differ, since each is humanity? They are, of course, one. If they do differ one from the other, therefore, they will do so only on account of some addition to one or the other; in that case neither will be absolute humanity but a sort of humanity, something human rather than humanity itself. And since each will partake of the same humanity, each will likewise be called human; and it will also be humanity in itself, a single humanity, before it is subjected to multiplicity.

It is true that since God is simply the cause, He should not be called the Maker of a particular man or of a particular horse, but the Maker of man and horse. This is why He created one single Idea for each type of creature. But among us, when one man begets another he should not be described as the unqualified begetter of man but as the particular begetter of a particular man. For the man alone is not the cause, but he is within the cause, that is, within a number of causes; and he does not do everything, since he does not supply the primal substance or the soul, and he does not give origin to the man himself; for man was universal prior to this particular man and, regardless of his particular activity, man is universal and will be universal.

But when Plato says that God has begotten a single Idea, either because He did not wish there to be many or because there was some necessity that there should not be many, you should understand that with God necessity and will are interchangeable, so that something is necessary because God wills it so, for in the supreme simplicity of the Godhead necessity is nothing other than will. If, therefore, you say that it is necessary for God to will or to do something, I shall change this to 'God wills that this is necessary'. Of course, where supreme goodness meets supreme power, that is where supreme freedom meets supreme necessity.

At this point there are some disparate but highly useful statements to be considered, such as 'Reading or study is useless if it does not lead to excellent conduct of life'. In this regard, the life and practices of Pythagoras aroused admiration from all, as rightly did his great authority, even in the time of Plato. Again, 'If the harmonious composition of words be removed from poems, the poems lose all significance.' Or, 'The virtue of a man or thing consists in a certain ability to move principally towards that end for whose sake the thing has been made and the man has been born.'

Meanwhile there appears to be some distinction between sense and reason, because the senses often make mistakes with regard to size, shape, number, and weight; but through its ability to measure, count, and weigh, reason corrects the assessment made by the senses. It is clear, however, that the soul is unable, through the same power, to make contrary judgements concerning the same thing at the same time. It is also clear that within us there are different powers of desire, for we may desire and reject the same thing simultaneously.

Note that it is not required of the upright citizen that he should suffer anything at all, but he should soothe the incipient pain with principles such as these, when it seems that there is one part of the soul which, as if sick, has need of medicine, and another part which, appearing healthy, is comforted.

But there are four main principles against suffering. The first is that it is not known for certain whether what happens is good or bad. The second is that, whichever it is, it is of little significance, for nothing is of great significance in the realm of human dreams. The third is that we advance not a whit through suffering. The fourth is that suffering always blocks that which can be of immediate help to us. This is confirmed by the fact that it is utterly disgraceful to be conquered, and eminently noble to be the conqueror; but the man who is oppressed by suffering or by some other distress has already been ignominiously conquered. For this reason his precept is that when there are adversities and disturbances we should assume the function of the doctor, not suffering with those in pain but healing them. He compares to throws of dice the everyday chances of life, which he wishes to rectify with these principles, just as the throws of dice are seen to be modified by some trick of the game.

But the precepts given earlier are like forerunners to those which follow. The greatest of all these is that what we meet in life is a contest in which we are to conquer vice and attain virtue, and that we should consider as nothing all those things which men hold good, in order that we may be good ourselves; for the true reward of justice is greater than all the trophies men may carry off, since the glory of justice transcends all these things beyond measure, and within the changeful, the fleeting, and the shadowy it is impossible to find the reward which is in conformity with the changeless, everlasting, and utterly true nature of justice.

The conclusion from this is that the changeless condition of justice must be yearned for as the unchanging reward, which abides in the undertakings of justice after the events of the present life. If this were not so, justice herself, who is judged to be the good that surpasses all others, would be something evil for just men who toil unceasingly from their love of justice and frequently suffer harm without returning ill for ill.

It should be added that, from their yearning for things eternal, they despise the good times of the passing moment and do not reap the reward due to men of justice, but in fact frequently receive unjust punishment for their devotion to justice. For this reason, to ensure that the good does not occasion harm, that justice is not without reward, and that God does provide and does recompense the worthy, souls are considered to be immortal, especially so that those unjust men who did not pay the penalty for their injustice during their lifetime should at least pay their debts after death, and that those just men who have been utterly despised by their fellow men may be crowned in the world above. Hence the words of the noble precept: 'The immortal soul must be painstakingly attentive not for this brief span but for time without end.'

51

Plato demonstrates the immortality of the soul in the *Phaedrus*, the *Phaedo*, and elsewhere. In the book *On Knowledge* he shows that there are definite proofs for such a principle, and he says that the words of those who believe the opposite turn out to be ridiculous when subjected to examination. Again, in *Gorgias* he declares that the mysteries have been proved with irrefutable reasons. And in this tenth book, after the discussion, he adds that this discussion and many other lines of reasoning compel us to admit that this is so. For my own part, I believe that within the words of Plato a wondrous power lies hidden, which very few appreciate, so that it is not surprising if Plato's lines of reasoning lead some to think that the case has been proved and others to think that it is still open to proof.

Demosthenes, who was undoubtedly a follower of Plato, was so moved by the power of his living words that after he had heard Plato and Xenocrates speaking on the immortality of souls he said he would rather die honourably than live ignominiously. This power in Plato's writings was also perceived by Cleombrotus and, in the Cyrenaic school, by many followers of Hegesias who, from their yearning for the next life, freed themselves from the dungeon of this body. It was also perceived by Boethius, a follower of Plato, who admitted, with Philosophy as his witness, that the immortality of the soul had been shown to him with sure proofs; and St Augustine seems to have intuited the same power, for he says that he has never had doubts about this matter. These things are confirmed by Avicenna, who says that there are principles which prove that this is so.

Not only does Plato say that this can be proved, but he says that it can be proved easily to those who, as I believe, have a mind that is purified and detached from the body, so that they do not doubt that at some time the soul is able to live apart from the body, since they find from experience that it is better for the mind to live apart from the senses than connected to them. They have also discovered that the souls of others which are buried within bodies and are therefore affected by vice do not perish from their own vice and disease and for that reason they are much less liable to be corrupted by some external or bodily ailment, since the body itself does not die from some external illness until the illness has been conveyed into the body, which is then very soon killed by it.

Furthermore, to ensure that no one doubts the divinity of his own soul, his prescription is that the soul should be thoroughly cleansed of the dirt accruing from love of the body and that, once it is purified, it should recognise its purity, its simplicity, its relationship with divinity, and the speed and fullness with which it is able to receive the divine light. But when he says that our souls do not increase in number with the passing days, understand him to mean that they do not arise from bodies or receive composite forms. This is made clear by the following principle, which says that if things divine are composed of physical bodies, the ultimate result would be that no trace of physical bodies would remain in nature, for things divine are never resolved back into physical bodies.

Note also his additional words, when he says that the soul is not composite, for if it were it would not be indissoluble. And understand that for essence to be indissoluble it cannot be composed of anything, or, if it be composed, it cannot be composed of any materials; it would need to be assembled in such a way that, within its composition, the multiplicity did not overpower the unity, for the unity, through its harmonious union, would need to transcend multiplicity, and stillness would transcend movement.

Bring these mysteries to a close, mysteries which pertain partly to providence and partly to immortality and the rewards of justice. The just man becomes like God, the unjust man unlike God. And since it is not hidden from God that the just man is like Him, and the unjust man unlike Him, it stands to reason that the just man is dear to God and is His friend, while the unjust man is the opposite. This is why God in no whit neglects the just, for they are His friends, but He always provides for them, so that all things, even the apparently adverse, turn out to be for their good, both in this life and after death.

But why at this point does Plato use an historical example, rather than carefully elaborated lines of reasoning, to declare the secret of immortality? It is so that the citizens may be spurred towards justice not so much by the skilful use of words as by an example and actual deeds. Again, why does he introduce, as confirmation of this mystery, a man who has risen from the dead? It is because, although immortality is firmly based on sound principles, as is the general execution of justice, it is useful to hear of the place, the form, and the arrangements for the dispensation of rewards and punishments from the mouth of someone who was present at the scene.

This is what the words near the end of the *Phaedo* mean to us. And his solemn declaration about Er of Pamphylia is not irrelevant: Er, who died in battle for the welfare of his country, rose again as a sign that those who die for the public good are resurrected to the true life, although only one of many was raised again to our life. But is this history, or a story? It is held to be history by Justin, follower of Plato and martyr for Christ. For my part, I shall not refute this.

But when Plato refers to a defence or a story, it can be explained that it is possible for an historical account to be called a story whenever it has some weighty allegorical significance beyond the scope of what actually happened. For this reason Olympiodorus, too, says that Plato frequently gave the name of stories to histories and other accounts. And since Plato locates the spirits of the dead and the seats of justice in one place according to the *Phaedrus*, in a different place according to *Gorgias*, in a third place according to the *Phaedo*, and yet elsewhere in this book, it is quite clear that these accounts have an allegorical meaning which extends beyond particular localities.

With reference to the resurrection he makes use here of the number twelve, which is the number of the spheres of the world in the view of the ancients, who think that above the four elements there are eight heavens, as if he were saying that virtue, the divine lady of the universe, is needed to raise the dead and that in the meantime the teaching is given to man by divine providence.

There are some who say that the great year, in which the soul of man completes its circuit and by which it returns to the same point, is comprised of twelve thousand years, and that three such years equal the great year of the world, in which the soul of the world fulfils its circuit through the movement of the firmament, thus completing thirty-six thousand years. They maintain that the circuit of our soul lasts twelve thousand years, because it has to pass through all the spheres and the ranks of daemons and gods, which, according to the *Phaedrus*, are arranged in twelve orders.

But what do they think is signified by the two openings in the earth and the two openings in heaven? It is that you may understand that souls descend to the earthly realm by one way, that is, by being clothed in an earthly body, and that they ascend from the earth by another way, that is, by being purified of that earthly garment. In the same way souls fall from heaven into the elements through love of the elemental body, and conversely they rise again to the heavenly realm when this love is extinguished and celestial love is kindled. Hence Orpheus says that love holds the keys for those above and for those below.

Plato says that the judges of souls are in the air, and he places the angels, ministers of divine providence, in the ether. After the sentence, the just go towards heaven, bearing their deeds and their judgements before them: for they know themselves and they shine for themselves as well as for others. The unjust, on the other hand, go downwards, bearing their deeds and judgements on their backs; for they do not know themselves and are of no profit to themselves, but are more of an example to others than a help to themselves. The meadow in which the souls rest for a while, both those which are ascending and those which are descending, is a middle region between the infernal and the heavenly, the attitude intermediate between good and evil, the state between bliss and wretchedness, likened to a zone in the air. Notice at this point that the souls which knew each other in the previous life recognise each other in the next life.

Again, according to the followers of Plato, the souls of those who died in infancy remain in such a meadow for a very long time, but Er considered that what was said of them was not worth recording, for they have not chosen to go into either region and they have not formed attitudes. The followers of Plato leave such souls in a light that is merely natural, but they consider that the blessed are placed above natural light, and the wretched below it.

Now there arises the question of the purifying punishments. But why is guilt eradicated by pains? Because it is implanted by pleasures. Do not doctors generally cure diseases with their opposites? Notice that Plato does not blindly use the numbers ten, one hundred, or one thousand for the removal of guilt. Indeed, for every degree of pleasure he applies ten degrees of pain. The first question is, 'Why do the degrees of punishment meted out exceed the degrees of pleasure that have been acquired?' The answer is that this is the penalty to be paid for a crime against the divine majesty. Moreover, just as the joys of blessedness exceed the pains of human justice, so do the torments of wretched injustice exceed the pleasures. In brief, it is not so easy to remove stains as it is to make them; and the man who has made a habit of sinning would not cease doing wrong if he were to live longer.

The second question is, 'Why ten degrees?' Has Plato taken his model from the ten commandments given by Moses? And has he thought that the man who has in any way broken any of the ten has somehow acted against the ten precepts of the divine law, and does he therefore judge him rightly to be tormented ten times? The number ten is accordingly said to be a universal number, for it either contains all numbers within itself or, by replicating itself and its contents, it will bring forth all numbers. Now the universal number is ideal for the purification of souls, signifying that the universal defect of the body must be laid aside before you can approach the Lord of the universe, in whose presence there can be nothing corporeal.

The third question is, 'Why, in addition to the ten degrees of punishment, are the unjust afflicted for one hundred years?' My answer is that if they had lived for a hundred years, which is the limit assigned to human life, they would have sinned unceasingly. Now to every ten degrees there is allotted the number one hundred, making one thousand all together. Hence the statements, 'They wander for a hundred years' and 'The wheel turns for a thousand years', and the other statement, 'You will receive a hundred for one.' For Plato uses these numbers not only in the punishments but also in certain rewards.

Indeed, if ten is taken into itself by multiplying ten ten times, the result is one hundred. Then if it is brought back upon itself through the calculation ten times ten times ten, one thousand is produced. Thus ten is a universal number, and one hundred and one thousand are universal numbers. Again, if you proceed from one to ten, a linear number results. If you move from ten to one hundred, the number is a surface. If you go from ten to one thousand, the result is a solid.

Thus, to give an allegorical explanation, the soul of the unjust man has departed from itself and gone into a body and is impaired by the stain of the body. The soul is going to be cleansed of this universal stain by means of ten, which is a universal number. The need for ten to be taken into itself, thereby producing one hundred, means that the soul needs to come forth from the body and return to itself through the use of reason.

Secondly, the need for ten to be taken back into itself to produce one thousand teaches us allegorically that the soul must not only turn towards itself through reason but must also be turned into itself through intelligence and thus be brought back to its own unity, by which it may ultimately be able to enjoy God, the highest unity of all.

Now the linear number, the plane number, and the solid number lead us mystically to the purification of the mind, not only at the outer surface of deeds, words, and thoughts, but also in the most thorough examination of those things that are very deep within.

After the intermediate zone and the region of purification, he goes down to the underworld. But understand that, according to the followers of Plato, there are not only temporary punishments in the region of purification but there are also temporary joys in a celestial region, in order that a balanced account may be given on both sides. For they make the following distinction. During life, either the senses are in complete obedience to reason, or reason is totally subject to the senses, or they are always battling against each other; and in that fight, sometimes the senses gain the upper hand and sometimes reason is victorious.

The souls, therefore, in which the senses comply with reason through confirmed habit attain everlasting reward, while those inclined in the opposite direction are condemned to everlasting punishments. But the intermediate souls are conveyed to temporary rewards if reason has been victorious, and to temporary punishments if the senses have been the masters; to them no time has been granted for deliberation. The followers of Plato see the intermediate zone as a place reserved for choice, and so it is called a meadow. Although some of his followers call the meadows the highest realms of heaven, here the meadows signify the airy region, for how could Plato here indicate the highest heaven by the word 'meadows', since he says, when referring to them, that some souls come down from the celestial realms, while other souls suddenly come forth from the bowels of the earth?

Let us therefore look upon such meadows as some lofty regions of the air, bordering on those lofty regions of the earth which he describes in the *Phaedo* as having the form of the earthly paradise, whose fortunate inhabitants dwell in perpetual springtime. In the same place they locate the Elysian fields: I mean the earthly ones, for the eighth heaven contains the celestial fields of Elysium. Hence the maxim, 'Heavenly beings and the forms of the gods alone occupy the stars.'

For the moment I briefly touch upon Proclus and Plotinus, both of whom, at the point where Plato says 'everlasting', speak of the whole time of the great year, in which occur the courses of all individual times. In this matter I commend Porphyry to some extent, and Iamblichus more so, for deducing matters eternal from this; for when Plato speaks of the incurable soul and that which can never be purified, he is clearly pointing to eternal punishments and, conversely, to unending joys. But the way some expound these matters I have not thought worth recording.

Moreover, if you consider the words of Plato, you will recognise that verse in the Gospels which says, 'Bind him hand and foot, and take him away, and cast him into outer darkness'. But Plato also speaks of the head being bound. Now the bond about the head signifies the obstruction to reason and the loss of sight, while the bonds on the hands indicate the loss of action and progress, and the bound feet cannot convey or move forward and attain but are paralysed by the removal of their power.

In the depiction of the fiery men you will also recognise the avenging daemons and the bodily punishments, and you will observe the same thing in many inferences. You will also mark the specific words used to describe the scene, in particular the darkness which ensues when the openings are shut, the groans, the gnashing of teeth, and the weeping.

But after he has arranged the places of punishment, indicated the places of joy in a contrasting figure, and touched upon the middle realm, he then returns to those souls which had assembled together in the meadows, some coming from heaven after a temporary reward and others from the earth after a temporary punishment. He says that they have to return to an elemental birth and through this they need to make sufficient progress to eventually merit a more stable condition or even an unshakeable condition. He says that they rested in the meadow for seven days. If you take this seven to be the seven planets, or the seven weeks in which the embryo rests in the womb before stirring, or even as the seven days in which forms in the womb gradually develop, you will perhaps seem to be making some contribution.

But how is this related to souls which are no longer in the planets? For they have descended, but they are not yet enclosed in the womb, since they are still to come down to it after they have been to the three Fates. In the meantime they inhabit an airy region by means of an airy body. Let this much be granted. Because they are living for this period in a kind of sterility, this may also be why they are designated by the sterile number; and since seven is not born from the repetition of another number and does not give birth to another number below ten, it is a very appropriate number to apply to souls which neither beget nor are begotten.

The followers of Pythagoras attribute this number to Pallas, for she was not born from a mother and did not herself give birth. They consider it a fitting number to give to souls which are still at some distance from an earthly mother and which are contemplating the universe by the wisdom of Pallas. But as soon as they arise from their respite they reach the number eight, which is born and which is also the first of the solid numbers; this is why it is very applicable to the soul which is moving towards a solid body. Now we call eight a solid number because it is made from two multiplied by itself again and again and indicating three dimensions, for two times two times two gives eight.

We may add that in music the seventh note is deeply dissonant, while the eighth note is fully harmonious. Now the body needs to be in harmony with the soul, and both body and soul need to be in harmony with fate, so that the celestial soul may have dealings with the earthly body. When the numbers of such harmony are finally achieved, the earth is in dissonance with the soul and the heavens are in harmony with the soul, provided that the soul is going to prosper.

Thus, because Plato adds to the eight days the four days needed for the movement of generation, you should understand that, within the nature of the lively soul, some power and disposition somehow exert their sway to form the body constituted from the four elements. Again, in the harmony of the eighth note, it is essential to have the fourth, which approaches harmony to some extent, and the fifth, a true harmony. They actually become five if you count the subsequent four with the preceding one.

And you will see, furthermore, that the number twelve has been allotted, so that souls may move to the early stages of generation. For twelve is the number needed to support the spheres and the ranks of gods and daemons. Moreover, the twelfth note and harmony are utterly perfect, arising as they do from the diapason and diapente, that is, from the eighth and the fifth, and being by their charm of one accord with creation and with marriages inspired by love. But such souls, under the guidance of the love instilled, so to say, by Venus, are now to be united through earthly marriages.

However, when Plato was about to count twelve and to add what remained to the number seven, why did he not simply say five? It was, of course, to hint, by means of eight and four, at those mysteries of which you have heard; and again, by the addition of one day's journey to make up twelve, you will notice that the body which is composed of the four elements cannot be prepared for the soul until it has been modified and put into a fifth form similar to the heavens and until the soul imparts from itself a life-giving imprint upon the impressionable body. But since souls which decline towards compound bodies are for the most part subject to the laws of fate, and, conversely, fall towards such bodies under the direction of fate, he says that the souls move into the view of fate.

He therefore firstly depicts nature herself as a column of light which is the chain of the universe. You should understand that life-giving nature and the power of seeds have been imparted to the substance of the world by the very soul of the world. It is called light because it penetrates and bestows life. Again, it is rightly called a column, because throughout its length it penetrates matter everywhere and produces many levels of forms which are then differentiated by type and kind. It is also said to extend in every direction and to bind the heavens in all places because it is wholly present everywhere and embraces everything and disperses many things as if through its sides, which are equal or similar to each other, but in such a way that the length is the same as the breadth, for it spreads out by penetrating, and the more it spreads the more it fills, and as it fills it rules. Hence the saying: 'Spirit nourishes within.'

The different colours denote the different powers of the seeds. There is no doubt that within this nature lies the spindle of the Fates: this is pictured as the axis of the spheres which befits the twin poles and the centre; but according to reason, it is an image of the world-soul, the life-giving power which watches over the nature of the world-soul and moves it like an instrument to produce the things of nature, not only artistically but also inexorably, so that in the cosmos there is not only an order arising from nature but there is also an inevitable order arising from fate. Hence the words in the *Statesman*: 'The cosmos is guided by natural desire and by fate.' The kinship of nature with fate, however, is so close that philosophers can scarcely distinguish one from the other. But to express the immutable nature of fate, Plato says that the spindle is of adamant, while the whorl, or heaven, is of adamant and other substances: the stars both fixed and moving and having a great variety of forms.

It is clear, then, that the number eight represents the spheres which are moved by nature and which are also moved by fate, the overseer of nature; and these spheres are said to be the instruments of fate. Many points are driven home here which relate to the measures, the depths, the intervals, the movements, the harmonies, the forms, and the powers of the heavenly spheres, and we shall expound these more appropriately in the commentaries to the *Timaeus*. But, in brief, you need to understand that from the extremely rapid and ordered movement of the heavens and from contact of great power there is produced a melody of great intensity and variety and of the utmost sweetness, the lower notes arising from the slower movements, the higher notes from the faster movements, and the intermediate notes from the intermediate movements. But since rudimentary hearing lacks the spatial relationship needed to appreciate the heavenly melody, such sound is not heard.

We consider that here there are the nine Muses and the Sirens: the eight notes of the spheres and the harmonious combination of all the notes. He says, accordingly, that the spindle of fate, that is, the extent of time, turns between the knees of the goddess Necessity. Her three daughters are Lachesis, Clotho, and Atropos, who, together with their mother, turn all things heavenly. I pass over the views of Proclus, who posits not only Jupiter as the one universal maker of the whole cosmos, but three more Jupiters under him as minor creators. Then, to correspond, the one goddess, Necessity, watches over everything at that level at which the universal Jupiter creates everything. In addition, there are the three Fates, that is, the three goddesses who are the daughters of Necessity: it is by the authority of their mother that the different daughters keep different things far from erring. And he places the goddess Necessity entirely above the cosmos, but he puts her daughters at some distance from the cosmos and partly inclined towards it.

But I and many other followers of Plato prefer to see Necessity as the soul of the cosmos, and her three daughters as the three powers of this soul which pertain to what is ordained by fate. However, he calls her Necessity not because she inflicts violence on nature or on reason, but because she preserves everything within that realm which has been assigned to her by the Creator and because she does not allow anyone to transgress its laws so far that the transgressor cannot speedily return to those laws.

Plato locates the heavens at her knees, that is, at her lowest part, to indicate the great ease with which she fully and freely enjoys all the while the bliss of contemplation. But he gives three names to this life-giving part of Necessity: Lachesis, because she is heavy with the seeds of creation and with the lots and forms of lives which she proffers to the souls as they are about to descend; Clotho, because, with her thread, she spins the lots into the act of living and puts them into effect; and Atropos, because she preserves and guards those lives which have now been unwound into action, as they move inexorably towards their inevitable end.

Some give the name Vesta to the first, Minerva to the second, and Mars or Martia to the third.

Then when Plato says that the Fates sing to the harmonious movements of the Sirens, understand him to mean that the powers of the Fates take effect through the movements and influences of the heavens. The thrones of Necessity and her daughters indicate the inflexible nature of the thread of fate, as if the movements of the movable are necessarily ruled and ordered by the immobility of the mover.

But the equal intervals between the thrones clearly show that a just distribution is made among the Fates and through the Fates. The white robes of the Fates indicate a nature that is both pure and blameless; for their nature, depending as it does on the supremely good Ruler of the universe, never does ill to the universe. Their garlands signify their authority. Their singing, through the intervening periods of time, shows how they arrange all things with that harmony with which the divine mind, through immediate observation, ordains all things to be governed in due season. Hence it comes about that the Fates all sing of particular times.

But why does Lachesis sing of the past, Clotho of the present, and Atropos of the future? Let Proclus answer. He says that the three times are considered to be in the past, for what is now past is said to have been present at some time, and before it was present it was future. In the present, the present itself is considered as future before it has been. In the future, the future alone is acknowledged.

Then the characteristics of Lachesis are made known; Clotho holds the second place of honour; and Atropos holds the third.

But why do the Fates turn the spheres with their hands, while their mother does not? This is because the lowest parts of that soul are more akin to the spheres than is the substance of that soul. Why, again, does Lachesis touch them with both hands? This is because the middle and the end are contained in the beginning. And why does Clotho take hold of the larger orbit from the outside and turn it with her right hand, while Atropos holds the smaller orbit from within and with her left hand? This is because the unfolding of life through its intermediate stages begins from an external cause, and the fuller it is the more prosperous it is, while the inevitable end arises from an inherent characteristic and finishes in restriction, as well as creeping up stealthily and, in most cases, against one's wishes.

But when Plato says that the Fates touch the heavens from time to time, you are not to think that the fateful powers of the world-soul rule worldly matters on some occasions and do not rule them on other occasions, for if there is changeability within fate, whose characteristic is immutability itself, it will be impossible to imagine anything that is unchanging. Plato, therefore, depicting divine functions in a human way and with human language, wishes to suggest that the Fates handle some matters and not others.

This is because the power of the world soul, being firmly based on the excellence of its own integrity, applies its action to the things that need to be governed, and while doing this it does not combine with anything else; it is also because the Fates reveal a temporal alternation in their works, and any intervals which they are said to have in their operations are shown in the effects and not in the Fates themselves; and finally, because Plato is dealing with natural things he does not touch upon things that are higher than nature, for he does not deal with those things which pertain to pure, free reason or to the divine intelligence, since such things are related in a wondrous arrangement to the sublime providence of God, which is higher than heavenly Fate.

The *Statesman* likewise declares that the affairs of the world are governed sometimes by Fate and sometimes by Providence, not because such a change occurs through some intermittent alternation of the times but because every day some things occur under Fate and some are ordered by the laws of Providence, which are higher than the sequence of the events ordained by Fate.

Moreover, our souls are at times wholly within the embrace of Providence, at times directly within the scope of Fate, and at times in both simultaneously. For when they live only with the mind that is unhampered and contemplative, they live only in Providence and with total freedom; but when they live in the life-giving part, then the inclination towards this body and towards imagination grows strong and spreads, they tend downwards towards Fate, and thus they fall away from freedom. Yet while they are conjoined to the composite body, they sink into the very destiny of this body and retain almost nothing of their former freedom. In short, after they have gathered the bodily dispositions together into a constitution, they are now completely overwhelmed by Fate and deprived of all freedom.

It will be asked here why souls seem to move towards Lachesis through some natural impulse. There is no doubt that, within nature as a whole, bodily instruments are the seed-forms of all species, ready to germinate not only with particular forms and in particular ways but also in due season. Indeed, within each specific nature and the nature of every species there is a similar seed arrangement designed to propagate and preserve the individual species. Within every individual of the same species there are similar potentials and inclinations to produce specific things in the appropriate ways and at the appropriate times. These three natures are henceforth so disposed that the individual follows the species, and the species follows the genus, with the result that, in most cases, that which is of the nature of the one is of the others too, and any particular nature accords with the general nature.

On exactly the same principle is Fate, that is, a template for the development of creation within the soul of the world, within the souls of the twelve spheres, within the souls of the constellations, and within, as it were, particular souls, numbered among which are the human souls. Within the life-giving power of our soul there is, therefore, some specific fate and a coiled-up series of future events which accords in shape, manner, and time with the fates of the heavenly souls and of the world soul.

Thus, just as the shoot of every plant, sprouting into specific shapes in its own season, seems to concur spontaneously with the universal nature of springtime, which calls it forth, so souls by their own nature and their own fate manifest specific lives at favourable times when universal Fate sends out such a summons, so that the chorus of souls, with its figures of dance and the diverse forms of its different dances, reflects the song and speech uttered by Fate. I should prefer the song to be understood to be within the heavenly souls, the speech within the spheres, and the dance within us.

Prompted by this impulse, souls reach Lachesis, at the beginning of life, to have their individual lots confirmed through the lots of Lachesis. They are thus confirmed through a prophet. 'Prophet' means two things here: the universal and primal influence of Providence upon the soul, and the opportuneness which provides that congruence whereby souls are borne to that to which they are borne by universal Fate. Therefore, when the prophet says that the souls are placed in order and that the lots are transferred to them by Lachesis, his meaning is that all these things are confirmed both through the goodwill of Providence and through the opportuneness of that congruence.

And it was not beside the point to say that the Fates govern the universe with their hands, while the lots of the souls are received from the knees of Lachesis. For since the governing of the universe is more important than the disposition of souls, it is deemed to be effected by hands, while the disposition of souls is carried out with knees. Being seated on a dais is a sign of authority and judgement. But between the lots of the lives and the examples the distinction seems to be that the lots pertain to the quickening powers, while the examples pertain to the imaginative powers, which exceed the quickening power but are at hand.

Indeed, within this power, as soon as some of these seeds of the future life grow strong before others do, at the same time the forms and devices of a similar life rise up into the imagination, and the emotions are stirred, just as, within us, the sanguine disposition of the body is followed by a cheerful imagination, the choleric disposition by a wrathful imagination, the melancholic disposition by a sad imagination, and the fertile disposition by a licentious imagination. This is as far as the necessity of fate reaches.

But reason is higher than imagination and is characterised by ratiocination, deliberation, and choice, and this is why free movement towards both, acquiring the configurations and dispositions of the imagination, can equally approve and disapprove of the plan for such a life. And this is why he says that virtue is exempt from fate, while blame for the choice of a worse life lies with the chooser and not with fate. For although it is initially in accordance with fate that a new life is chosen in general and in particular, it is from one's own deliberation that this life or that life is actually selected. Indeed, if reason based on examination rejects the first form of living that is presented by the imagination to the eye of reason, another and a better life will imme-diately appear, followed by yet another. This is why this inspiration of Providence is called prophetic, for by some illumination of the judge-ment it informs reason that it has the freedom to deliberate and to choose and it shows the main consequences of a heedless choice.

It is also stated that a prophet pours out the lots and presents examples of living, not only because the influx of divine Providence sanctions to some extent the workings of fate but also because it presents, for reason to examine and judge, the lots ordained by fate and the examples arising from fate. But when the herald announces that souls are 'of a day', he is declaring that they are there for an unbroken day and that the life which they esteem so highly is but a day and a night. He adds that a new cycle will begin, in order to disclose the mystery of the souls moving from heaven to earth and back from earth to heaven.

He says that the human race is not only mortal, but, in order that souls may have a presentiment of their own ills, he adds that it also carries death, as if he were saying that the life of the body is the death of the soul. He then announces beforehand that, although reason is free from the beginning in the choice of life, once it has made its choice it is no longer free to reject what it has chosen; and yet it will be free at times to order and modify it in various ways, whatever kind of life it may be.

If you ask why the souls of men choose various lives, some people will reply that the differences in the natures of souls are governed by types, and others will say that they are individual and even personal, adding that many differences are derived from the diversity of the previous life. Plotinus strongly supports this view and fully harmonises it with what follows.

And so the souls that choose a life are immediately allotted a daemon as the guide for the life they have chosen. We have spoken a great deal about this elsewhere. Here let us make the following distinctions. The followers of Plato consider that some gods are outside the world, minds detached from the body, such as the intellectual spheres, worshipping the one God as their immovable centre and their unshakeable unity. They call others the world-gods, transcending divine worship and being favourably disposed to the turning spheres of the world. Below these are the daemons, ministers in the arrangement and composition of those things which come into being either within a type, or within the spheres, or even outside the spheres. They say, therefore, that there are as many kinds of daemons as there are powers within the world-gods, the leaders of the daemons. But in truth, within each of the world-gods, the unity of its substance, the link with divine unity, is the highest element.

After this comes the intellect, which observes all things simultaneously and through which the angelic minds are made available. Next there is reason, which extends by a sort of forward movement and is a particular property of such souls. Then there is a kind of imagination which moves through particular forms, just as reason moves through universal forms. Next comes the nature, both quickening and moving, of the life-giving sphere.

To complement these five powers there are reckoned to be five kinds of daemons. Of these, the celestial daemons fittingly accompany the unity of the world-gods, while the ethereal or fiery daemons accompany the intelligence of these gods, the airy daemons accompany their reason, the watery daemons their imagination, and the earthy daemons the nature which, within the gods, we have called life-giving.

Below these the followers of Orpheus place the subterranean daemons, which are related through the lowest order to the bodies of the world-gods and which are the avengers of crimes. Plato seems to have spoken of them here.

If you ask which daemons in particular are the guides of the souls which are coming down into bodies, the answer will be that they are not the heavenly ones or the fiery ones, for these, being higher, do not bring the souls down but take them back. Again, they are not the watery daemons or the earthy ones, for these, being the producers of the lowest creation, do not lead the soul on the journey mapped out by fate but hurl the soul down into the chasms of fate. The airy daemons thus remain as the intermediate guides through the intermediate realms, the companions of divine reason leading human reason along this journey.

Different daemons of this kind guide different souls: the daemons of Saturn guide Saturnian souls, those of Mars guide Martian souls, and so on, each daemon corresponding to each soul in mental disposition, providence, and fate, and particularly in relation to the form of the life that has been chosen.

Then, with this daemon as the guide of life, the souls now approach the three Fates, which they had merely glimpsed previously, and thus, with the establishment of the daemon as the executor of the whole sequence, and with the gradual preponderance of the physical disposition, they finally move past the three Fates to the mother of the Fates. This is Necessity herself, whose influence they now experience.

Then the movement of the souls through scorching heat has three possible meanings: firstly, that the ardour of physical love is growing, and at the same time care and anxiety are increasing; secondly, that they are moving down from heaven through the sphere of fire; and thirdly, that the agency of natural warmth is needed to give life to the earthly body. But since it is through excessive care for earthly matters that matters celestial are consigned to oblivion, and since it is through oblivion that barrenness replaces fertility, they soon go down into the barren plain of Lethe or oblivion.

And because they cherish mortal things and thus cease to care for things eternal, a situation which produces oblivion and deprivation, he says that the souls of the plain of Lethe go right down to the River Amelita, which is the lowest level of heedlessness, and there they lie down at night, which means that they are laid prostrate through being cut off from the divine light.

But what is the meaning of the statement that the waters of Amelita cannot be held by any vessel? This is, in fact, a poetical metaphor to show that base matter, which is called a river, flows and surges unendingly through all forms. It also shows the defect of oblivion, which is to retain nothing but allow everything to drain away immediately. It further shows that there is no external support which can prevent the soul from perishing through its own heedlessness. That it is necessary, moreover, to drink from the river of oblivion is clear, because it has been so decreed by the nature of the individual, by fate in general, and by Providence. But whether a soul drinks more of the water or less depends on how inclined it is towards the body, and this is why there is more oblivion or less, more power of recollection or less.

Let there be no doubt that the soul experiences these mental dispositions when it is within a body that is made of the thicker air at a higher level and before it is enclosed by the womb of an earthly mother. For the downward journey from heavenly to earthly bodies passes not only through the airy element but also through an airy body. Plato adds that the soul sleeps in this airy body until the middle of the night, thereby indicating that in the earthly body the night of ignorance will be total and not partial. The sleep itself indicates both the obstruction to reason and the erroneous nature of the soul's judgement.

Finally, he says that the souls find their way into an earthly embryo at a time of thunder and earthquake. I believe he has two reasons for saying this: firstly, to show that they enter this dungeon under unfavourable auspices; and secondly, to show that strong movements, both celestial and earthly, need to combine in order to force the divine soul into such a foul prison-house. But their shooting upwards, like stars, towards their birth goes beyond a poetical figure by suggesting that the souls are somehow stellar and that they will eventually return to the stars.

However, the fact that Plato presents such a laughable tale, just like those spun by old women, about the transmigration of souls into the bodies of animals reminds us that the whole account needs to be expounded allegorically, with the explanation that rational souls do not transmigrate into the lives of brutes, but into a brutish life, that is, into a life similar to that of a brute; and the converse is also true. This is the understanding that is fully accepted by all the followers of Plato, with the exception of Plotinus. And Origen, in his books *Against Celsus*, seems to confirm this view.

However, to prevent you from being heedless of the moral principles, the expertise of right choice needs to be given precedence over all other matters and skills. Moreover, so many things have been presented here about the beauty and power of the spheres that we may consider that justice will win a great prize in heaven and that it will lead most surely to the best way of conducting one's life.

Yet you will now say, magnanimous Lorenzo, that you have received from Marsilio Ficino a commentary rather than a summary. Let there be no doubt that I consider that it has been worthwhile and that it will remain worthwhile for me to have provided a commentary where I had promised a summary.

PART TWO

The Commentary of Marsilio Ficino
to Plato's *Laws*

The Theme of the
First Book of the *Laws*,
dedicated by Marsilio Ficino
to Lorenzo de' Medici

M AGNANIMOUS LORENZO, in the view of the ancients there
was a single period of time in particular which held three very
bright lamps of wisdom: Pythagoras, Socrates, and Plato. We have
found, however, that the wisdom of Pythagoras puts greater emphasis
on contemplation, while that of Socrates stresses action and that of
Plato gives equal weight to both contemplation and action.

Moreover, the contemplative discipline of Pythagoras and the moral
discipline of Socrates both seem somewhat remote from the common
customs of men. But the teaching of Plato, which is both speculative
and moral, seems to provide a universal marriage of the divine with the
human, such that it can easily adapt itself to the common customs of
men and at the same time turn men to things divine and eternal.

Yet it should not on this account be thought that Plato diverges from
Pythagoras and Socrates, whom he reveres as divinities, but rather that
he combines them and tempers their divine power, if I may use such a
phrase, to the human condition, so that it may to some extent be said
that within them was a purely divine power, while in Aristotle and the
other philosophers who followed Plato there was a merely human
power, but in Plato the power was equally distributed between the
divine and the human.

Why should we mention this? So that we may remember that
since the arrangement of the *Laws* under consideration is given to us
by Plato himself – not through the person of Pythagoras or Socrates, as
other things are, but simply through the actual person of Plato himself
– it is right to keep to a middle path between things divine and things
human, so that we are not dragged through unknown or impassable
ways or drawn down to the realms below. This is why the ten books
of the *Republic* smack more of Pythagoras and Socrates, while the
Laws now under review are deemed to be Platonic. The *Republic*

73

arrangement was for those who would desire and choose a Republic, while the arrangement we are now considering is for those unable to make such a hard ascent.

They will not, at any rate, refuse to approach these gentler slopes. Consider how much care Plato gives to the welfare of humanity, for he wishes to seem not only admirable in men's eyes on account of the lofty heights but also simple and kindly and beneficial to all on account of the lower slopes. Thus he will not compel men against their will to have all things in common amongst themselves, but he will allow individual men, according to the custom, to have their own property.

Yet our extremely careful charioteer will not in any way slacken the reins. For, in addition to the supreme care displayed by the other laws, he will decree most wisely that no one is permitted to enlarge his property beyond a fixed modest limit, lest some have too much, while others have too little and many be obliged to be beggars in the arms of their mother-land, a condition he considers to be quite wretched.

The fact that the person of Plato is discreetly concealed under the designation of the Athenian stranger will later become clear to the reader for many reasons and especially because he is going to declare that he has dealt with twin republics. But when he is going to establish laws for the Greeks, he rightly takes the laws from the best three founders of Greek laws – Minos, Lycurgus, and Solon – pruning, adding, modifying, and devising; and thus, from all of these, he produces the best possible form.

And although at the outset he determines the State and the rule of government, yet he refers to the giving of laws rather than to the Republic, for in that State in which property is held by individuals many laws are necessary to deal with a variety of disagreements, lawsuits, and offences.

You will mark the admirable and most merciful disposition of the divine Plato in establishing these laws. For a man noted for his kindness devises an inspiring introduction to each law which will attract the people in such a gentle way that they will be perfectly willing to obey the law, and, by their own choice, like children of the laws, they will conform to those which others obey unwillingly, as if they were obeying tyrants, shunning their dominion either by subterfuge or by violence. But after speaking at great length, he does add threats, and even punishments, for those who consider their homeland as a step-mother and not as a true mother.

Let us now turn to the real subject of the first book of the *Laws*, once we have advised everyone to read the dialogue called *Minos* and its summary before approaching these laws. They should approach them, I say, with the intention of diligently observing them in their decisions and faithfully keeping them in their actions. If this is not the case, and they will not obey them, they should understand that after such a precise presentation of justice and injustice they will be guilty of the minor and the major transgressions.

The Athenian stranger, that is, Plato, having gone to Crete, is near Knossos when he lights upon Megillus the Spartan and Clinias the Cretan, whom the people of Knossos had invited, together with nine others, in order to bring a settlement from there, to found a city, and to give it laws.

These two, therefore, were making their way to the sacred cave of Jupiter for consultation on this matter, when the Athenian stranger met them and enquired what they were going to do. They answered that they were going to devise laws. But when the stranger asked them many questions about laws, they were scarcely able to reply; and since the stranger seemed to them highly qualified in matters of law they besought him to go with them as their helper in administering a State with laws.

The stranger therefore complied and first of all laid before them the principle from which and through which laws have come to men, namely, God and the philosopher. Then he enquires into the aim of laws, teaching that such an aim would be the untroubled purity of the hearts and minds of the citizens through the contemplation of truth until it is fully complete. Thirdly, he considers the actual form and content of laws.

The evidence that laws are breathed into men by God is supplied by the whole of antiquity, by many of Plato's books, and by the reasons adduced in many of our summaries of the Dialogues and confirmed in our *Theology*, whenever religion is discussed there. Indeed, if nature, being nothing but the lowermost instrument of divine providence and appearing to tread prudently wherever she goes, is not her own guide, but is guided by providence, which ordains within itself the purposes and arrangements of all things and assigns them to nature in the way it sees fit — if nature, I say, does not overflow with excess or suffer a deficiency of what is needful, then it is certainly the case that divine providence is never deficient in what is needful.

One necessary provision for the human race is the incapacity to live except as a harmonious society. Law is also needed for society, which will quickly perish if far removed from law. In turn, what is needful for the laws is divine authority, lest they fall into disuse through negligence or are infringed through deception or violence. But what is needed for the establishment of divine authority is holiness of life and a penalty that surpasses human power and strikes awe into everyone.

This is why the providence of God, which foresees what is needed to meet the respective requirements of all the kinds of elements, plants, beasts, and members of society, and does so with much greater care in the case of that most perfected species of living beings which worships the Godhead, cannot be deficient in sanctioning laws which are particularly pertinent to the welfare of human beings.

He adds that no leader, without the breath of heaven, can bring to harbour the huge ship of State, which at any moment may be buffeted by storms and is at the mercy of countless perils.

And so, whenever necessary, God reveals the mysteries of laws through the unmanifest inspiration of souls and openly sanctions and promulgates them through manifest miracles. For this reason Plato begins his work on the *Laws* with invocations that are true and felicitous, appropriately calling three times upon God at the very outset. For these three lawgivers hold a discussion, and they all stand in need of divine protection.

These three also follow in the footsteps of the authors of laws – Minos, Lycurgus, and Solon – who refer laws to three divinities: Jupiter, Apollo, and Minerva. And this is quite right, for the Sun, which is the Lord of the Planets, holds power, while Jupiter is filled with mercy, and Minerva with wisdom. These three embrace the whole nature and perfection of law.

For do we say that law is anything but the rule of reason which leads its subjects to the Good by way of a certain order? To ensure that reason and rule and order are inherent in law, wisdom is absolutely necessary. To ensure, moreover, that it achieves its end and is pre-served, power first enables it to lead to the Good, that is, to the welfare of all; and to ensure that its way is agreeable and kindly is the principal provision of mercy.

And so, according to the ancients, the three deities representing the divine trinity are inevitably responsible for laws. And for this reason three comparable gifts are deemed necessary in a leader for the administration of the laws. And since it is necessary for these perfect gifts to work together in establishing the laws, which is something human ability cannot effect, divine assistance is required to establish the laws with the utmost precision.

Since Plato, in *Minos* as well as in this present dialogue, often refers to a nine-year period as being necessary for inwardly receiving the laws from Jupiter and conveying them to men, he may be pointing to the nine orders of angelic minds, through which, as if through interpreters, the very reason for the establishment of law may be passed on to men.

In *Protagoras* he subsumes all these orders, which are the interpreters of the laws, under the single name of Hermes. And, of course, you are not unaware that this number nine in relation to angels is used not only by Christians but by Platonists, too, especially Proclus and Syrianus, as we clearly show in the *Theology*.

What should our conclusion be, then, if nine indicates here the threefold use of power, the threefold nature of wisdom, and the triple nature of mercy, but that the number three is within the law, within the judgement of the magistrates, within the servants of the law, and within the execution of the judgement?

Moreover, the number three is within the beginning, the middle, and the end of all things and of all actions. And three times three clearly produces the number nine.

But why is the beginning of the discussion in the *Republic* based on what is sacred to Minerva, while here it is based on what is sacred to Jupiter? Is it because the discussion in the *Republic* takes place in Athens and concerns the ancient city of Athens, which is dedicated to Minerva, while the present discussion occurs in Crete, concerns the building of a Cretan city close to the very temple of Jupiter, and begins by speaking of the laws of Minos, the son of Jupiter? Or is it because the earlier form of the State was purer, stricter, and fully appropriate to Minerva, while its later form was a little more kindly and closer to Jupiter in its gentleness?

In short, both in this dialogue and in that, we invoke a blessing on the emerging State through prayers and sacrifices.

I pass over the account of the long journey, the sacred groves, the trees dedicated to the temple, and many other things, all of which would be better suited to a commentary than to a summary.

But after some words which teach through allegory that human affairs, especially those which are public, cannot be rightly arranged without divine guidance, and that this is why the beginning of the laws is the worship of that Jupiter who made the world and gave laws to the world and to us, it is right for him to deny at once that the end of the laws is the worship of Mars, at the same time making some modest adjustments to the laws of Minos and Lycurgus because, instead of looking at simple virtue itself, they have tended towards the warlike aspect of virtue.

Indeed, the laws should particularly consider as their end in the State that to which they direct all things as if to a standard which, above all else, needs to be sought out by all citizens. But the battle and the victory, being full of toils and evils, are not to be chosen for their own sake but for the sake of peace and the full tranquillity of life, for no one chooses to live in such a way as to be constantly fighting against ills and triumphing over them.

He concludes at length that it is fitting not to relate the arts of peace to martial activities but, on the contrary, to relate martial activities to the arts and to works of peace, and peace itself to the free and unhindered worship of truth and God.

But in demonstrating these things he apportions the nature of good things into many species, saying that some things are human, while others are divine, and that things human depend on things divine; that of things human, which he judges to be far below things divine, the first is health, the second is beauty, the third is strength, and the fourth is wealth, while the leader of these good things is prudence, which is also the leader of things divine. After prudence, in his judgement, comes temperance, followed by justice, which in its turn is followed by courage.

In fact, what he means here, and what he expounds in the fourth book of the *Republic*, is that there are three parts of the soul, the rational, the spirited, and the appetitive; that prudence is within the rational part alone; and that courage is within the spirited part alone.

But he places temperance and justice in all three parts together, and he names both temperance and justice the harmony of the whole soul. Yet temperance is the harmony in the emotions, while justice is the harmony in actions. Temperance is the health of the soul; justice is the beauty of the soul; prudence is the eye; and courage is the hand.

If you consider the substance of the soul and the purity needed for contemplation, you will put temperance before justice. If you consider human custom, you will put justice first. But you will certainly put prudence before all others, just as you would put the eye before the feet and consider it as their guide. You will put courage before continence, for courage is not so easily deflected and at the same time it encompasses within itself both the endurance of pain and the function of continence, which is to overpower desires. Both are deemed lower than temperance and justice, which control the entire order of the whole soul as constituted by prudence as its guide and leader. From this he deduces that the lawgiver should himself relate, and cause others to relate, things human to things divine, and things divine – the virtues – to a mind dedicated to truth and to the nature of the divine.

But while discussing the end of the laws, he also expounds the duty of the lawgiver: and his meaning, in brief, is that he should cultivate the whole State with the utmost care, like a field, and with an excellent system for selecting and sowing seeds, for the appropriate cultivation of every kind of plant, for the immediate rooting out of weeds and thorns as soon as they appear, and for bringing everything to maturity in due season. But in all this take note that the man who succumbs to pleasures is considered worse than the man who succumbs to pains.

Again, the duty of the courageous man is not only to overcome fears and dangers but also to curb his passions. Moreover, no one can be truly accounted courageous unless he has undergone long, hard exposure to toils and perils and, we should add, unless he has successfully passed through the trial of licentiousness and the allurements of pleasure in which those who are truly self-restrained are tested.

Note that it is not safe to train a man to be courageous when he is far removed from fears, or to train a man to be temperate when he is far removed from all the allurements of pleasure. Moreover, the active study of the lawgiver should centre on pleasures and pains, so that these two, like brutes, are not without a bridle. For if they are restrained by a bridle, it is easy for life's journey to become happy. If there is no restraint, the journey becomes very difficult and unhappy.

You will note, too, what is said about the Athenians: the upright Athenians are particularly upright, because they alone are upright by their own nature and by some divine dispensation, without any coercion or threat. What Plato means when he says this is that in a badly organised State good citizens, though rare, are the most excellent of all men, for without any training they have emerged as they are through some divine dispensation and the perfection of their nature, and their excellence is such that they are not contaminated by the general contagion.

Next, you will consider the following guidance for each art and for the whole of life: those who have shown themselves to be most outstanding from their tenderest years in practising and attending to any art must be viewed by the instructors of each art in such a way that games most appropriate for manly accomplishments are offered to the boys, and thus the souls of the players will be most strongly drawn to a love for that sport which they will practise seriously when they become men.

It is at this point that discipline is defined. Discipline is that training for life from earliest childhood which leads the soul of the child, step by step, to the love of virtue, that virtue in particular, I say, by which he knows, on reaching manhood, how to command and how to obey.

That a man needs to have and is able to have such a discipline from his tenderest years Plato aptly confirms with the following description of human nature: for he says that although man is a single entity he contains within himself many diverse elements, among which are two tyrants, loving and yet opposed to each other, thus distracting the soul. They are Pain and Pleasure.

In addition, there are thoughts of future good things and of future bad things, of which desire and hope arise in us for the good, while fear of the bad also arises, and there are similar disturbances of the soul. There is also the judgement of reason, declaring which of these is better and which worse. Now such a judgement in an individual is a private law, but in the State it is a public law.

Yet since he said that one living being was composed from such diverse elements, he pertinently adds that of all living beings man is a divine miracle, and he follows Hermes in saying that man is a mighty miracle. Living beings are of three kinds: for either they are immortal in body as well as in soul, or they are mortal in both body and soul, or they are immortal in soul but mortal in body. Of the first kind are the beings that are celestial, ethereal, and airy, be they named gods or daemons. Of the last kind are the brutes. But of the middle kind are men, watery daemons, and earthy daemons. For since the bodies of these daemons are composed, as are human bodies, of opposites, they can be dissolved at any time, and they spread disturbances.

But if all else is set aside, why is man a miracle? He is a miracle because, although he is divine, the wonder is that he is infected with mortality; and on the other hand, although he is mortal, the wonder is that he has affinity with the divine.

But why is he called a divine miracle? Because he is so ordained by divine providence; and, as *Timaeus* teaches, we have received from God, the Maker of the world, the very substance of the rational soul, while from the other gods we have received a vital nature that is lower than reason, and finally, from the daemons, we have received physical bodies.

When he adds that man was made by the gods either for play or for earnest application, you should understand him to mean that man was made for play if the soul, in its perpetual movement from things heavenly to things earthly and from things earthly back to things heavenly, as if in play, never comes to rest with God in His unchanging abode; whereas man is said to have been made for earnest application if only the soul will remain unchangingly at some time in the presence of the creative gods and of God the Creator.

Which side we should choose in such a division Plato does not venture to declare here. However, he considers it probable, as he indicates both here and elsewhere, that man has been divinely constituted for a degree of serious application rather than for play. But anyone wishing to interpret these ambiguous words of Plato to mean that man has been constituted by divine beings should understand this to mean 'by the stars'; and anyone who interprets it as saying that man is composed of many creatures should understand that the parts and affections of the soul are being poetically called 'living creatures' by Plato. This is made quite clear in the ninth book of the *Republic* and also at the beginning of the *Phaedrus*. But you will have seen these passages for yourself.

Plato then moves on to things which, although seeming less serious, are necessary to the perfect passing on of discipline and good ethical standards: the study of music and similar pursuits. Now music, through its universal meaning, includes the ordering of all proportion, not only in speech, song, sound, and dance, but also in gymnastic sport and the grace of the convivium. All of these things need to be arranged in such a way within a State that, with every incitement towards disturbance and vice removed, they will temper the body, the spirit, and the soul.

However, he begins the discussion in a congenial way with banquets and wine, saying first of all that care must be taken to ensure that drunkunness does not reach the agitations which are inherent in us.

For if drunkenness makes its intemperate entry, it inhibits the functions of reason and adds to the onrush of agitation. Yet he approves of the convivium and the taking of wine, once this caution is heeded, a caution which he will explain more fully in the next book. But for the present he deems it best to convey the point that sometimes a too liberal consumption of wine reveals men's habits at banquets, for it usually makes men more shameless and reckless.

In this matter, therefore, the wise guardian of the youth, restraining the vices of young people, especially the vice of shamelessness, will be able the more easily to correct the youth and promote in them the habit of preserving a sense of shame even in the most shameless drunkenness possible.

How great the shame is, is evident from the fact that it is on account of such fear that young men are most afraid of anything disgraceful and that they boldly approach whatever is honourable, even if it be daunting.

These two things are indeed judged to be more necessary than anything else to a Republic, both in peace and in war; and for this reason the lawgiver must energetically apply himself to infusing these things into the hearts of the citizens.

The Theme of the
Second Book of the *Laws*

OUR PLATO, through his wonderful love for the human race, leaves nothing untouched in his discussions which may seem in any way to be conducive to the welfare of mankind. And being intent on pursuing it, he would rather err on the side of prolixity and inquisitiveness than on the side of neglect.

Thus, in the second book also, he examines the carefully chosen discipline imparted to those of tender years; for, observing that children, rather like wild animals, have almost no values but will rush to wherever pleasure attracts them and flee at once from wherever pain deters them, he quite rightly sets a charioteer over the horses of childhood, to hold the reins of pleasure and pain, before the unfortunate tendency to rush forward or to run away hardens into habit.

This charioteer he calls discipline or virtue, which first reaches children, as far as pleasure and love and pain and hatred have a good influence upon their minds, before they are directed by their own reason; later, when reason is present, they submit to their own reason as a result of the right practice of good standards of behaviour.

He sees this universal submission as virtue, while he gives the name of discipline to that enhancing practice related to pleasures and pains by which men hate those things which it is right to hate and love those things which should be loved, and do this from the very beginning of their life to the very end, for as long as their life is governed by the reason of another. But then, when the man yields to his own reason once it has been aroused, he calls this by the name of virtue.

Even Aristotle himself, in his *Ethics*, strongly confirms that the basis of a moral life of this kind is of the greatest importance. But since children are restless by nature, seeking amusement in all things and being therefore not amenable to harsh discipline, Plato directs that children be brought up with that universal music's honourable pleasure which proffers the hallmarks of virtue; and he goes so far as to direct the same for older people from time to time, for they need some honourable delights to be presented to them in compensation for their life of toil.

It is certainly for this reason that he says that the gods, moved to compassion by men's life of toil, appropriately instituted rituals and festivals sacred to them in order to alleviate men's toils. In fact, they appointed the Muses and Apollo and Bacchus to lead these celebrations, with the aim of removing any blemishes from the jollity of men's customs and of moderating the grasping nature of emotion by means of the musical proportion of movements, so that their delights might be honourable.

These words, however, not only praise the divinely approved and vouchsafed use of music but also teach allegorically that on many counts man would be more wretched than the beasts if he did not undertake, through divine providence and divine affinity, the practice of divine worship and religion. In this matter the Muses signify the divine discovery of truth granted to religious people by God; Apollo signifies the pleasing expression of this discovery, as well as prophecy; and Bacchus signifies abstraction of mind and the admirable work of religious men.

Note that harmonic proportion has been bestowed upon us particularly by divine providence, that through this proportion we might harmonise all the movements of our restless nature which of themselves would be inharmonious. From the Muses we have harmony in the movement of our soul; from Apollo, harmony in the movement of our speech and song; and from Bacchus, joyous harmony in the movement of our limbs.

Yet while he carefully discusses this musical training which is wholly relevant to children, but also pertinent to older people, he repeats what he has posited in the *Republic*, namely, the regulations by which licence to give expression as they will is never granted to poets, musicians, and painters, for they are to express only honourable and serious subjects that will benefit those who look and those who listen. But he will have, as judges of the expression, men who are experienced and full of gravity, and he directs that, through an honourable expression that is resorted to every day, the young men should continually encounter, in all their games and pursuits, those very things over which the laws and the elders rejoice and lament. Indeed, he deems that such acquaintance is the whole basis of virtue.

At the same time, commit to memory some things that are fully conducive to the rules for good living.

The unjust man, even if he possesses all that men consider good, is unhappy, and as long as he is alive it should be said that it is better for him to die than to live. Again, whoever has separated the honourable, the useful, and the pleasant, by speaking of them separately, is not to be heeded. And although the honourable and just life can sometimes appear toilsome, this is never to be communicated to the children; on the contrary, they should be told that the most perfectly just life is the most pleasant of all.

Plato maintains that this will be necessary, although it may seem otherwise to those with whom he is contending. And he calls for silence at this point. Truth, however, is something beautiful and constant.

He then comes right down to the taking of wine, which he wishes to be completely unknown to young men before their eighteenth year. When this is not the case, he says, fire is poured upon fire, as much in the soul as in the body. After this age he allows the moderate drinking of wine. But after the fortieth year he grants that, at banquets, it may be liberally consumed between hymns to the gods, as if it were a remedy against the harshness of old age by which we appear rejuvenated, and we are overcome by forgetfulness of all vexation and by the love of spirit, just as iron becomes more malleable once its hardness has been transformed to softness in the fire.

In this way he would have it that the older men, who would otherwise refuse to sing, would wish, on becoming more cheerful at banquets, to sing to the ears of the younger men and at the same time, as we might say, enchant their souls. By such enchantment the souls of the younger men would be tempered through the gravely harmonious melody.

As you read these words, you will note that grace itself is called beauty within objects and it is called delight within cognition. You will also note that no creature apart from man has the sense of rhythm and harmony and that rhythm is order in time and movement, while harmony is order in the very tempering of the notes by means of high and low. What we often call harmony is properly called *concentus* in Latin. What we call rhythm we can conveniently call number, provided that you understand this to mean number in time and movement.

You will note in what respect wine is useful and the care with which it is to be drunk by those present at a banquet, be they lawgivers or guardians, sober observers of the customs of drinkers, correcting the customs and, when they have been softened by the wine, appropriately reforming them.

He concludes in brief that if the citizens, with these restrictions, consume wine at banquets it should be admitted that wine is useful in relation to what has been said, but its consumption for individual pleasure should be stoutly denied to the citizens, for it is a most shameful disturbance to the citadels of Pallas, which should be revered before all else.

The Theme of the
Third Book of the *Laws*

JUST AS A DOCTOR looks to the health of the body, so does the giver of laws look to the health of the soul. But since it is more desirable for all to retain good health and not die than to receive good health while dying, the prime duty of both the statesman and the doctor is to preserve health, be it of the body or of the soul. Their secondary duty appears to be to restore the body or soul to its best state, if this has been lost.

This is why, according to Plato and according to truth itself, those who draw up laws are deemed worthy of censure if they are quick to discern the censure by which crimes should be punished, but do not provide the means by which men may be so raised, nurtured, and instructed that they have no desire to commit crimes.

No one, therefore, will be surprised that in the books of the *Laws* and in the *Republic* our Plato, in his eagerness for the unfailing health of the soul, dwells rather carefully on many points which seem of little importance and which concern the training of children and young men. For it behoves the scrupulously diligent doctor of souls to act in this way and to prepare them, from their very birth, so that they seem to have been born with good health, or at least so that the health of their soul is settled by the time they are young men.

Hence the first and second books of the *Laws* emphasise diligence in every kind of music and sport and also at banquets. For when he discusses the duty of the lawgiver, he judges that the first thing to make clear is the lawgiver's prime concern for children and young people.

At this point I should like you to remember how careful he was in measuring out the wine to be drunk, judging it wrong for it to be drunk every day or by everyone or as the individual pleased and restricting its consumption to august banquets only, and then by grown men and in moderation. As for undiluted wine, it should be used on rare occasions and under the guidance of a regulator and judge.

You will also recall his strong insistence that wine is not to be drunk by soldiers in camp, by slaves in the State, by magistrates or governors, by judges at the time of a trial, by men on the point of making momentous decisions, or by any man or woman at a time when they choose to devote their attention to begetting children.

It is worth committing these things carefully to memory.

Let us now proceed to the real theme of the third book. Since, therefore, law itself is a form of government, that is, of civic discipline, while government is a form of citizenship, it is not irrelevant for him, at the outset of his treatment of the laws, to hold a lengthy discussion on the beginnings of citizenship and government.

But he is unsure whether the human race has existed from eternity or not, and he is equally uncertain about the world. And when at one point he describes time as endless, he certainly does not mean that it really has no beginning or end, but rather that it is endless according to our methods of reckoning; and this is why he often describes time as incalculable rather than limitless.

Again, he expresses his view with the same uncertainty in the sixth book when he says, 'Either the human race had a beginning or it began at a time incalculably earlier than ours.' But perhaps he says 'incalculable' to prevent anyone from trying to reckon up not only the solar years, but also the lunar years, and the days and hours.

However, it is sufficient for a Christian that the Philosopher has not affirmed the eternality of the world. But what will the followers of Moses say about a thousand years when compared to these thousands? Perhaps they will say that Plato, following the Egyptian tradition, used extremely short years in his reckoning. But a discussion of these matters and of the world deluges is to be found more appropriately in the *Timaeus*.

At this point let us revert to the actual substance of the *Laws*, that is, to citizenship and government. Four types of government in particular are enumerated. The first type, immediately after a disaster befalling the human race, is found in some survivor, his seed being preserved by the help of extremely high mountains or, rather, by divine providence. For it is then likely that the sons and grandsons are ready to heed the authority of the head of the family. Such authority, in fact, rests solely on the laws of nature.

The second type of government is that existing among several families which have banded together, within a town or some similar fortified place, from some common need or from fear of wild beasts. But from the very beginning of such a union it is likely that there have been as many forms of governing as there are households, forms that are very different one from another in opinions and customs. The injustices springing up among them on account of such diversity have compelled them to appoint common arbiters, judges, and governors.

From this the third type of government has arisen, having its origin in the previous injustice. But it is probable that these city governors have ordained laws in common for the State, after considering the most honourable laws obtaining in the households, and through these laws they have transferred the discipline of the household to the discipline of the State.

The fourth type of government lies in the rule of peoples, when numerous cities join together in a common will and law, just as many families unite in one city.

The first type of government is outside the city, operates through individual laws, and is based on nature, reason, and will. The second type is within the city, operates through the individual laws of households, and is based on some common need or fear. The third type is within the State, operates through common laws, and cultivates justice when injustice appears. The fourth type is a combination of many States and operates through a common will and law.

In these matters the poets are urged to sing divine songs, for it is said that the race of poets is divine and is prompted by God. The lawgivers, too, are urged not to impose laws that are harsh or aggressive, but laws that are light, so far as is possible, and agreeable.

Moreover, through an historical example, the main purpose of this discussion is pursued on the subject of the distinctive and best principle for the giving of laws, which has its origin here in particular, if the lawgiver, when giving the laws, looks to that universal virtue of the citizens which is the greatest of all the virtues and their leader. But no one doubts that all other virtues are governed by prudence, just as the less important limbs are governed by the head.

That prudence is as fully vital to us as it is noble he confirms from the fact that all people, with a common desire, have it as their prime wish that all things should happen as they would choose and have the outcome that they would choose; and they consider the happiest man of all to be the one for whom all things happen according to his desire. But Plato draws the opposite conclusion: the most wretched man is the one with whose desires events concur every day, unless the man is endowed with so much prudence and, through prudence, rules his mind with such moderation that he can discern what is truly good and can yearn for those things which he has distinguished by reason, to the neglect of all else.

Here he is urging us to long or pray, not that everything should be in accord with our desire, but that our desire should be in accord with reason.

He also makes a brief but apt comparison: as a son is to his father, so is the father to God. A boy certainly desires as many things as possible to happen to him and he welcomes them as good, while the father sees them as evil and prays that they do not occur. In the same way, the heavenly Father continually rejects men's prayers if they are empty or harmful. We have no safeguard against deceptive prayers except for prudence.

The lawgiver, seeking the happiness of all, will make his prime objective the cultivation of prudence in the minds of the citizens. For the excellence of prudence is that it teaches us to desire and obtain what should be desired and shows us how to most profitably employ what has thus been obtained. In this consists the entire prosperity of the State.

But just as prudence preserves the State, so does imprudence, which he calls ignorance, destroy it. This is not ignorance of writing or of some art or of things external and strange to us, but ignorance of the Good, as he often says in other places and as he means here. But he adds that this is, both individually and collectively, utterly harmful ignorance, by which a man does not know how to moderate his own soul in such a way that his disposition, like a people lawfully brought up, obeys the laws of reason, its queen, so fully that what he pursues and shuns, what he rejoices in and grieves over, and the way he does so, is all as the dictates of reason prescribe. Any who are blinded by such ignorance, even if they are very gifted and learned men, are considered ignorant by Plato, while those who are temperate are judged by Plato to be prudent and knowledgeable, even if they are unlettered.

He then forbids the power of magistracy to be granted to any man who, through lack of restraint, is unable to govern himself. Again, he does not believe that a State can be rightly and prosperously constituted under a man whose soul is in a chaotic and wretched condition.

But although he proceeds to list seven principles which are deemed to be among those most conducive to the high honour of governing – namely, fatherly care, excellence, lordship, power, age, prudence, and fate – he himself selects prudence alone above all the others, saying that this is the principle befitting the high office of command: those of greater prudence should hold sway everywhere and should temper those who are less prudent.

Just as the function of the eyes is to guide, while that of the feet is to convey, and just as in any skill, but especially that of the sailor, the soldier, and the physician, the duty of the man with greater understanding is to direct, while that of the man with less understanding is to perform, so, within the art of citizenship, which governs the individual, the family, and the State, all must give their first allegiance to those who understand the chief factors conducive to men's welfare.

Law, therefore, seeking prudence for all, will ensure that, in addition to childhood instruction conducive to prudence, the levels of public offices will be universally allocated in accordance with the levels of prudence itself. And to ensure that the reins of power are not handed over imprudently, the law will not allow the sheer unrestricted power of control to be granted to anyone, but it will subject everyone to the laws, while uniting the rulers with the senate, and the senate with the views of the people.

It will take heed, first and foremost, that arrogant licence, wishing to have greater power than the laws have, does not engender dissension and destruction. It will take pains to ensure that the whole body of the State, as far as possible, is free, prudent, and well-disposed: free, so that all can care for their country; prudent, so that all will know how to care for their country; and well-disposed, so that all will wish to care for their country.

It will remember that these three factors are united with greater ease in that State which holds the mid-point between the power of one and the power of the people, so that it does not subordinate itself totally to the will of a single ruler or to the power of a few men, and does not accept any adviser indiscriminately, but is based on government by the best and has both a royal element and a democratic element.

It will carefully consider the customs and fortunes of the leaders, in order to ascertain that the destruction of States and kingdoms arises principally from the effete and immoderate life-style of the youths and the men. Indeed, since it is impossible for anyone of outstanding virtue to emerge from such a life (for it will make everyone ill, weak, puffed-up, and blind), it will therefore require everyone to cultivate temperance most of all, and it will decree that those should be honoured most who, in the judgement of all, are acknowledged as the most temperate. It will not allow anyone to have fortitude without temperance, for this would be extremely dangerous for the State, and, indeed, extensive experience without justice would also be very harmful.

But to state the matter briefly: if the gifts of the soul have been mixed with temperance, it will accord them the first place of honour, it will subject to them the good things of the body, and it will command what is external to serve the good things of the body and of the soul. It will not allow excessive freedom or excessive domination, for the latter destroys friendship (which is both the goodwill of the people towards the leader and love for one's own country, so that either the leader or the country may perish through some trivial cause) and the former engenders licence first, then scorn for the laws, followed by constant insurrections and, finally, by total domination.

But no one will be surprised that, both in this dialogue and frequently in others, Plato assigns great importance to sports, or rather to the arts of music, as if they were most effectual in bringing about a complete change of life both communally and individually. For in those days such arts were well known to everyone and were frequently practised quite publicly; but what is practised continually by everyone has no less effect upon the soul than air has upon the body. Besides, the things that are considered trivial by those physicians who lack circumspection are believed by Plato, that most observant physician of the human race, to be things that should never be slighted.

Then he summarises his earlier statements. In this summary the words beginning 'But if anything …' could perhaps be read as 'But have we conveyed anything, or not? Who will refute this? For everything has been spoken between us. But you will have seen these things yourself.'

The Theme of the
Fourth Book of the *Laws*

THIS FOURTH BOOK, like the three preceding ones and also the first part of the fifth book, focuses on the purpose and function of the lawgiver.

His purpose relates to the substance and form of the State. This substance is the position, composition, and disposition of the city.

The form is the method and arrangement of civic government. But since this form can never be beautiful unless the souls of the citizens are beautiful, the lawgiver is commanded to watch over the shaping of the citizens' souls from their tenderest days and throughout their lives.

Plato therefore expounds the substance of the State in just a few words, but he deals very precisely with its form and with the moulding of the citizens' souls, like a man who puts no value on any external things, even though they seem vast, in comparison with the worth of men's souls.

Indeed, if our Plato were a doctor of bodies he would take great pains to choose the most salubrious air as being conducive to the steady, robust disposition of the body. But a man who, in choosing an Academy for himself in a healthful position, has been guided not by the body but by the soul and by good ways of living, certainly appears more than moderately careful when founding a city; and when moulding ways of living as well as a new generation, he seems, if I may put it like this, to be diligence itself, like a doctor of souls.

Moreover, if he were to value the good things of fortune as highly as others generally do, he would carefully seek out productive land, a good location, and the most convenient way of piling up wealth and extending his power. But he does nothing of the sort. Therefore the city should be far from sea and harbour, not given up to commerce, especially retail trading, or to excess, and not wealthy. Let the State be temperate, sober, undefiled, and, most importantly, full of piety.

What do you think any holy pontiff will entrust to the religious life when building temples and the habitations of the saints, other than what our Plato directs in the founding of a city? And the man who here says little about the body of the city says nothing at all about the founding of a city, in that blessed Republic which he portrays in ten books. And there is nothing amiss in this, for he has left that Republic in heaven and is building this one on earth to be, as far as possible, an image of that model Republic.

The lawgiver's resolution will therefore be to give little importance to anything other than the welfare of the soul, in favour of all that benefits the soul, and in every instance of instruction to aim at the target of universal virtue. And for this reason he will not allow anything in the State or in the environs of the city whereby the citizens could ever fall into bad habits, even if the outcome were to be victory over many peoples, vast power, and all manner of things in abundance.

For the law directs its attention not outside the soul but into the soul, to bring it to perfection in all respects. It will therefore ensure that the citizens do not give the highest priority to the prosperity of this false life, and that their care is not to live and be well so much as to be very good for as long as they live.

But Plato considers that three factors above all are conducive to the implementation of the lawgiver's resolution: God, fortune, and art. These three are said to govern the whole human realm. And for a man who lacks patronage they are more difficult than for anyone else.

But when Plato says that God, fortune, and art linked to God govern the whole human realm, his words can be briefly explained like this: God, within all, moves all through all. He moves the spheres of the world. The meeting of the spheres is elsewhere called fate, but here it is more happily referred to as fortune. From fortune proceed the various conditions which befall external things and bodies. God also moves souls by filling minds with light, whence are kindled both the art of reflecting and the art of acting. Finally, from art proceeds the configuration of external things and of the body.

For these reasons, all things depend on God, who, as Saint Paul says, works all things in us. But from God Himself some things proceed through fortune, and others through art. Hence it comes about that neither fortune nor art ever has the power to resist God, since they are, in fact, both moved by Him at all times.

But the relationship between the two is such that either they agree with each other or they disagree. If they disagree, either fortune triumphs over art, or art overcomes fortune. Here is an example of what is meant. While God is moving the spheres, there are occasions when, through fortune, He stirs up a storm at sea. The storm shakes a ship. At the same time God is moving this ship through the soul of the helmsman, that is, through art, which is ever dependent on God. Thus when art directs the ship towards a particular harbour, and the storm also bears the ship towards the same harbour, then art and fortune agree together. But when the wind drives the ship in one direction, while art strives to guide it in another direction, then art and fortune are in disagreement; and eventually art yields to fortune, or fortune yields to art. Meanwhile the providence of God acts in both situations and leads to an end known to Him alone, with whom nothing is ever in disharmony, for in mysterious ways He moderates all things in the universal harmony of His work.

Moreover, when that arrangement of celestial encounters is such that it will necessarily prevail over art, it is called fate rather than fortune; but when it is such that it can overpower the indolent and be mastered by art, it is then called fortune. And you should not doubt that there are times when art can conquer fortune, for both fortune and art proceed from God.

But note that when Plato discusses the moment chosen by a great man as most propitious for establishing new laws, he indicates Dionysius the Younger by the name 'that well-known tyrant', and he indicates himself by the title of 'lawgiver', and he shows that he has none of fortune's favour. Again, Plato began the prefaces to these *Laws* when staying with Dionysius in Sicily, as can be understood from his letters, but he completed the work on the *Laws* after Dionysius had been exiled. Lastly, through these words he justified his return to Sicily on the basis of madness.

But you should know that on that journey out and back Plato was seeking only for a violent tyranny to be changed into a moderate monarchy, whilst preserving Dionysius' good fortune. At the same time, however, when he speaks of the temperance and prudence of a prince, you should remember that Plato clearly distinguishes moderate temperance from prudence, and on the same basis he distinguishes moderate prudence from wisdom; but he often describes perfect temperance as prudence, and occasionally he refers to perfect prudence as wisdom. There are many such instances in *Phaedo*, the third and fourth books of the *Laws*, and in other places.

In addition, he adduces some natural talents which are akin to the virtues and which, when rightly cultivated, are conducive to the gifts of the virtues. Plato discusses this matter more fully in the *Republic*.

Meanwhile, you will commit to memory the fact that the ways of princes become the ways of all the citizens. And this is the quickest and easiest means of changing the ways of the citizens.

Again, Plato is a happy, prudent, and temperate teacher of the people, and the people are also happy, because they hear the words flowing forth from the mouth of such a teacher. Moreover, the State will not be happy and no good laws will arise until power in the ruler conjoins with wisdom and temperance. Therefore divine aid should be invoked in the formation of a State.

To this point the fourth book has dealt rather generally with the function of the lawgiver in relation to the substance and form of the State. But from this point onwards it proceeds to a clearer definition of this function, and it asks whether the State should take the form of a monarchy, an aristocracy, an oligarchy, or a democracy.

But since nothing good can, in fact, be spoken from one man to another unless what is said reflects the divine Good, Plato is right to explain the form of divine governance before declaring a preference for some forms of human government when compared to others, that is, when he is going to put government that is like divine governance indisputably before all the others.

Now he shows that divine governance is monarchy, and aristocracy conjoined with monarchy. He thinks that from all the citizens there should be chosen as governors those who excel all others in prudence and temperance to the degree that men excel boys. And if anyone among those chosen excels all the others to just the same degree, he is to be appointed king. But this can be clearly seen from the present mystery of Saturn, as well as from similar words in the *Statesman*, the *Letters*, and the *Republic*.

Besides, in order for the present mystery of Saturn to be understood more fully, it needs to be remembered that the followers of Plato infer that the world is preserved and guided by life and soul. For this inference they draw on three principal items of evidence: the strong bond connecting the varied parts of the world, the wondrous movement of the heavens, and the unceasing generation of things beneath the heavens.

They also conclude that the world is ruled by mind through the threefold order which is observed in the bond that unites the parts of the world, in the movement of the spheres, and in the generation of things. Our celebrated Platonist succinctly embraces both soul and mind: 'Spirit nourishes inwardly, and Mind, pervading the interstices, impels the mass entire.' Lastly, they conclude that both the soul and the mind are directed to rule by the Good Itself and the One, and they base their conclusion mainly on the fact that the connection of the parts and the movement and generation and the entire arrangement of these three move towards the One and are directed towards the Good.

This is why, beneath the Good Itself, a dual rule obtains: that of the intellect and that of the soul. All the ancients call the first the rule of Saturn, and the second they call the reign of Jupiter. The ancients portray Jupiter as usurping the reign of Saturn because although they both call souls to their respective kingdoms – Saturn to the intelligible good, Jupiter to the perceptible good – very few souls betake themselves to the intelligible good of Saturn, while vast numbers stream unceasingly towards the perceptible good of Jupiter and a life of action.

The ancients tell us that souls once lived in bliss under the rule of Saturn and that their understanding operated in two ways. The first way was when they lived among the divine and angelic minds, before they slipped down into bodies. The second way was related to how frequently and in what numbers they devoted themselves with burning love to the contemplative life, despising the life of pleasure and paying very little heed to the active life. But whichever way is taken, souls are happy in the intellectual life and miserable in the creaturely life.

Moreover, they are so deceived in this misery that when two planets are in the heavens, the first being the messenger of the higher Saturn and the second being the messenger of the higher Jupiter, they praise the star of Jupiter but pour reproach upon that of Saturn; for the first calls one on to good things that are transient, while the second calls one back to things eternal. But since man, as a social animal, cannot, if separated from the general dealings of mankind, maintain a middle way of life and is obliged, if I may put it like this, either to go down below the level of man or to rise above this level, the situation is such that Saturn, the separator of men, has become an object of reproach and infamy, a scapegoat in the minds of the ignorant, who through some absurd confusion or twisted upbringing have emerged as beings which, when they are withdrawn by Saturn from the level of men, go downwards from this level rather than upwards.

But we have written in greater depth elsewhere on these matters. Let us return to the main theme.

Plato adds that Saturn once divided men into companies and entrusted them to the guardianship of daemons. Now this can be explained in many ways. One explanation is that, in the beginning, the divine mind, as Timaeus says, divided the souls of men into various orders to accompany the number of the souls of the stars. Some followers of Plato think that what differentiates our souls one from another is merely to do with number, whereas others consider it to be related to type, their view being that our souls belong to a single genus, within which there are many types of soul, and many souls within a single type. But however they may be organised, souls are said to be adapted not only to various stars but also to various daemons.

The mystery may be explained in another way: from the beginning of the world, or immediately after the Flood, uncultivated men were governed by the divine providence of angels or by the ministrations of the better daemons until the time when, gradually acquiring more experience, they were able to govern themselves. But it is consistent with reason that men are governed more properly and more profitably by higher beings than by themselves.

A third explanation is that those who every day choose the principle of life (which is in some way kept remote from others) and have been rightly brought up are said to move at once into the contemplative and blessed kingdom of Saturn. But the more they are differentiated into varying observances through their practices of contemplation, the more they appear to separate into numerous flocks and, in conformity with the similarity of the life they follow, to be inspired and ruled by the appropriate deities.

For the present I make but passing mention of the many schools of outstanding philosophers which are like flocks miraculously gathered together under Saturn, their shepherd. They are under Saturn, I say, in three ways particularly: firstly, they are under the divine angelic mind; secondly, they are under the soul of the chief planet and its sphere; thirdly, they are under the body of the planet itself.

But the mind enacts, the soul prepares, and the planet portends. It portends, I say, when, in the great conjunctions of Saturn with Jupiter, Saturn himself rejoices in his own exaltation or in his house, and as the lord of the conjunction he is cherished by Jupiter and he enjoys the beneficence of the Sun, of Mercury, and of Venus. Thus he gave birth to the magic of Zoroaster and his followers or, rather, he portended their teaching, as well as the theology of Trismegistus, the mysteries of Orpheus, the secrets of Pythagoras, the pure virtue of Socrates, and the grandeur of Plato. From clear lines of reasoning we know that this is so.

Hence, in the present book, Plato affirms that Saturn is the lord of those who possess mind, and he shows that the rule under Saturn was royal and for the best, for he asserts that the human race was governed by God Himself, as though He were the king, through excellent daemons that were carefully selected. Many people call them angels, and in *Critias* Plato calls them gods; both in *Critias* and in the present dialogue he points to the ease of government, saying that men were once governed by some secret inspiration of conviction and that they should also be governed in this way and should receive guidance whenever they abandon the lower inclinations and submit themselves to the higher ones.

Plato is thus teaching us, firstly, that divine providence is never absent from human beings, provided that they are not absent from themselves; secondly, that human nature becomes lustful and domineering when given absolute freedom and power; thirdly, that just as animals cannot be ruled by other animals without some human guardian, so men cannot be ruled by other men in the best way unless God be their guide, and, while some mortal rules without God, life will be toilsome and wretched, as if to say, 'Except the Lord keep the city, the watchman waketh but in vain'; fourthly, that the disposition of the mind is the law, and that obedience should always be given to this in all aspects of government, both private and public, so that through our own mind we may be happily guided by the divine mind; fifthly, that no resolutions are to be called laws unless they procure the general good of the whole State; sixthly, that the powers of magistracy and, most of all, the offices of divine worship should be granted to those who are punctilious in obeying the laws; seventhly, that destruction has been laid up for that State in which the laws do not rule the magistrates but the magistrates rule the laws; eighthly, that the young see these things through eyes that are quite beclouded, while the old perceive them with clarity, unless perchance God on occasion gives His approval to youthful piety or His disapproval to the impiety of the elders.

Plato has now said a great deal to instruct the lawgiver on his duty.

From this point onwards he addresses some words to the people who are to receive such laws, that they may welcome them the more gladly and keep them the more earnestly; yet he exhorts them first and foremost to observe the sacred laws and through these laws to observe the human laws which have been revealed and confirmed by the divine. But to his exhortation he adds veneration and awe, saying that God, the Creator of the whole world, embraces all within Himself and thus looks into the hearts of all, lest any man trust that he can conceal his transgression; and he declares that God permeates everything, lest any man hope to escape God's hands after committing an offence.

Plato shows that God is the founder of all laws when he says, 'He defines and enacts with a straight line,' that is, He determines all things by the straight rule of law. In fact, He first determines the measure for all things according to their individual natures: their kind, their number, their size, their place, their time, and their manner of movement. Then He determines what should be done by souls and what should be avoided.

It is indisputable that the application of such measures is the law for all things in the sight of God, the Maker of all, and that this is decreed by God Himself through that very act by which all things are known by Him and come into being: that circular act that Timaeus says is natural to the divine intelligence, which from itself looks back to itself and, by looking back, gazes unceasingly upon all things.

But perhaps in addition to the circular motion, which I might venture to describe as the motion closest to God, straight motion also finds a place: the outflow of creation from God and the inflow of God throughout the whole creation. This is why Plato says, 'He enacts with a straight line.' And he indicates that the straight motion depends on the circular motion.

Again, when he says that God holds within Himself the beginnings, the ends, and the middle parts, understand him to mean that God is the efficient cause and the final cause of creation, that He maintains all things, and that He is present in all things.

And to prevent anyone from thinking that the law is ineffectual he adds that it always goes hand in hand with judgement, so that those who keep the law and those who break it may be clearly perceived and what is due in particular to anyone may be effectively determined. And as judgement is readily distinguished and determined, there follow the inexorable retribution for transgressors of the law and the reward for those who observe the law.

But he says that the law is observed most punctiliously by those who most humbly bow their heads in submission to the yoke of the divine law, whose reward is judged to be future blessedness; and the law, he says, is spurned most of all by the proud, who are deserted by God once they have abandoned His law. Being deserted, however, they sin all the more abominably and are afflicted with even greater misery.

You, on the other hand, will keep these golden precepts of good tidings lodged deep in your heart.

But because he says that these mysteries are made evident by words uttered long ago, we can understand him to mean the words of Moses. We can also understand him to mean the words of Hermes and of Orpheus, many of which we have read on this subject, which are unmistakably clear, but which our present theme does not allow us to review more fully. Yet if you read the Orphic hymns concerning Jove, law, judgement, justice, and Nemesis, you will find all this word for word.

Plato next encourages the people, each and every one of them, to strive to be in the number of those who follow God, aiming to please God in all things and, in order to achieve this, making themselves like unto God through the purity of temperance by which, as by a rule, they may perfectly measure out all they have; for measure, as Pythagoras confirms, is considered better than all else, rendering the soul most like unto God. For God indeed is the measure of all things, particularly for us, who ought to pursue whatever is considered harmonious with the divine mind and will, and to shun whatever is not. This is why Plato writes in one of his letters: 'Law is God for the wise, while licence is God for the foolish.'

Although the text is doubtful at this point, in another place it reads as I have translated it. With these words Plato seems to refute

Protagoras, who says that the measure of things is man. Protagoras' error is clearly refuted in the book *On Knowledge*. But in another place the reading is not 'any man' but 'if a man', in this way: 'For us, God is the measure of all things, and much more, if, as they say, a man is.' These words — 'if, as they say, a man is' – could be expounded thus: 'If a man is the measure, God is much more so, for we ought to live not for ourselves but for God, through whom we have life.'

Another possible interpretation is: 'If God is a man', that is, 'If He were ever to become man'; 'as they say', that is, 'as the utterances of the prophets proclaim.' Would that this interpretation were as acceptable to the followers of Plato as it is esteemed by many people!

But so that it may be clear how much fruit accrues from observing the laws, he adds that only the observers of the laws have the right to offer their devotions to the gods and to perform their holy rituals, while the prayers and offerings made by others are rejected by God. In fact, he says that pleasing God is the target at which we must aim all the varied actions of life, as if they were arrows, and that the constant practice of religion is to ensure that the arrows reach God's mercy-seat.

In this practice he lists the same levels that we read about in the Pythagorean songs, for in both places he directs us, first and foremost, to worship all the heavenly gods, especially those patron deities to whom our land is dedicated, and then to worship the secondary gods below heaven, all of whom he calls terrestrial.

For although Plato, in heavenly fashion, locates all the elements beneath heaven and all those in heaven, it is his wont to classify all those beneath heaven by the name of earth, and all those in heaven by the name of heaven and fire. He regards the heavenly deities as the higher angels, as well as the souls of the celestial spheres and the souls of the stars; and he considers the earthly deities to be the lower angels and the souls of the four elements.

Thirdly, he enjoins us to honour the purer daemons as messengers of the gods to us. Fourthly, he directs us to honour the heroes, the souls of men acceptable to God, souls now separated from the body.

In all these matters, he ordains that the worship be so arranged that greater honours are bestowed on the greater deities, smaller honours on the lesser deities, and equal honours on those that are equal.

Fifthly, he wishes the statues of the ancestral gods which were devoted to the laws to be adorned and somehow respected rather than worshipped and adored; but since he laid the foundation for worship upon the one God, he showed clearly that other deities cannot be mentioned in their own right but only through their being part of the first God, and that they are not to be worshipped for themselves but for His sake, especially since he declares that the whole of such worship is to be undertaken simply in order to please that One.

Sixthly, he instructs us to honour our parents as God's representatives.

Seventhly, he says that we should follow the divine commandment and thus love, with unfeigned hearts, those related by birth or linked by family, as well as guests and strangers.

Moreover, it is ordained in the Gospels that a full reckoning for every idle word shall be made to the divine Judge, whose angel presides over us as the representative and minister of the higher Judge, to call us away from whatever is base and to urge us towards what is honourable, to nurture and delight the compliant with a peaceful conscience and to trouble the disobedient with a disturbed conscience.

When He gives delight, the ancients call it Grace; when He troubles, they call it Fury. And it is a threefold Grace, for the Grace of the past, of the present, and of the future grants delight to the good. Fury, too, is threefold, for it torments the wicked in a similar way. And in both cases fate or destiny is seen as threefold. It is also called Nemesis, especially by Orpheus, when it brings retribution to the haughty.

Indeed, in order to point out that pride, more than all else, is in opposition to God, who requires obedience in all humility, they said that the proud are punished not only by divine censure but also by divine wrath, and they established a deity specifically to administer this kind of punishment. He is called Nemesis, because he 'sheweth strength with his arm and scattereth the proud in the imagination of their hearts.'

Take four of these names in particular: law, judgement, justice, and Nemesis. Take what they teach into your heart. Remember the law, which declares as a general precept what is to be done and what is not to be done, stating that what is honourable is to be pursued, while what is disgraceful is to be shunned. On a clearer basis, you also have judgement, which discerns, through a review of the evidence, the honourable or the base element in this or that particular action. In the will you have justice, which elects to pursue or to flee, according to whether reason, through the laws of the mind, has judged it right to pursue or to flee. In the imagination and its emotional disposition you have Nemesis, which is angry and rightly impatient with base actions and words.

In the same way, there abide within God (but in a divine manner) law, judgement, justice, and Nemesis. But law abides more clearly within God and the higher angels; judgement within the reason of the world soul; justice within its will; and Nemesis within the lower angels or the middle daemons. However you arrange them, they all serve, through some amazing link to the divine law, to bring about reward for virtue and punishment for sins.

The Theme of the
Fifth Book of the *Laws*

EVERY DAY we can see the astonishing effects of the lodestone upon iron, of amber upon chaff, of lightning upon solid objects, of fiery brimstone upon bombards, and of the whole of nature in the movements of the heavens and the ingenious design of all that is born. We do not, however, know the causes, and yet we do not, through ignorance of the causes, deny the occurrence of the effects which we see.

That wonderful effects are also sometimes wrought by our souls upon prophecies and other marvels is attested by the whole of history as well as by the authority of Hermes, Pythagoras, and Plato. Although none of us can easily assign a definite cause to the astounding operations of our mind, yet we are not obliged to say that the operations have not occurred or are unable to occur.

We observe that fire has a closer resemblance to the heavens than do the other elements; that its action is so much more astonishing than theirs that in a short time it draws to its own form what the others take a very long time to draw to theirs; that it will not tolerate a compound substance; that when it seems to be divided it is dividing; that it prolongs its effect for much longer than do the other elements; and that by means of light it acts at very great distances and in a moment of time. It is indeed from heaven, and heaven acts through its image, that is, through light, which fire becomes through a property that is scarcely natural.

For who would doubt that the heavenly bodies, through their rays which are both hidden from us and obvious to us when they flow forth from the heavenly bodies as their images, continually move and shape all that is beneath them? In just the same way a mirror reveals faces, and a concave mirror removes dry material placed near it. But come now, within this mirror let us look into the soul upon the gods above.

As fire is more effective than the other elements, and as the heavens are more effective than fire, so spirits are more effective than the heavens, for they enliven and move the heavens and are the companions of all that enlivens and moves. Thus the higher spirits work upon our companions simply through the influence of their images, just as a face works upon a mirror; and by acting upon them they form and produce things that are very similar to themselves, so that souls often act just as wonderfully as the celestial spirits do.

But just as a mirror is equipped in five particular respects to receive images from the face – through its glassy nature, its clarity, its smoothness, its resistance, and its position – so our souls are equipped for the influences of the deities. Firstly, they are intellectual by nature, just as the deities are. Secondly, through the intellect, they cleave to the deities with undoubting faith. Thirdly, through will, they betake themselves to the deities with burning love. Fourthly, they place their steadfast hopes in them with the fullness of recollection. Fifthly, if they have a body which is naturally receptive to the deities and carefully prepared, then impulses come down to our minds from the gods above, and our minds are tempered in the same way that strings are tempered by the strings of the lyre. Then wonders, dreams, and prophecies occur.

I merely mention what Iamblichus and Porphyry relate: that some prophecies are made through water, some through air, and some through fire, perhaps because they are sent by watery daemons, airy daemons, or fiery daemons, and also perhaps because it happens from time to time and from place to place that the dispositions of human minds turn towards higher things and are thereby transformed.

In fact, our minds are pulled away in far too many directions, but whenever they are focused with full power upon a particular task, then just as fire consumes with the full power of its nature, and as the heavens act with all their influence, so impulses even more wonderful than fire and the heavens will arise from our minds. Of this Plato is sure, and so are Avicenna and Algazales, who are often, by some quirk of fate, considered to be followers of Plato. But we discuss these things more fully in the *Theology*.

The Gospel statement about faith moving mountains is strongly supported by these things and also by many more which Plato, in the previous book as well as in the fifth book, and indeed in all the subsequent ones, affirms with regard to prophecies, with the result that there is no organisation of a city, or formation of a State, or the sanctioning of laws without approval from the oracles. Yet although he mentions three oracles, he clearly gives his authority for this to other prophecies which can perhaps be considered more authentic. But let us now move on to the real subject of the fifth book.

Since, therefore, our soul is the mirror of the divine, it is right that after the worship of the divine described in the fourth book he should, at the outset of the fifth, ordain that the soul itself be worshipped as something holy; and the man who earlier copied the Pythagorean hymns is now also happy to follow his teacher Pythagoras in the worship of the soul.

After the gods, revere yourself most of all. How important reverence is to the observance of the laws is beyond my powers to explain, but its effect, if I may put it briefly, is that anyone who reverences the constant presence of his own soul as if it were a deity has a judge within himself: he governs his life in strict accordance with the law of this judge, even in the absence of written laws, and eventually, through love of the natural law, he finds it easy to perform what others, through fear of the written laws, have difficulty in performing.

When he is therefore discussing the worship of the soul, he communicates all the ordinances concerning duties that relate, on a personal as well as a public level, both to himself and to others in connection with all the virtues, the ordinances which each should learn and commit to memory. Here he puts an end to his introduction to the laws, at the point where it appears that the entire discussion concerning the laws is divided into three main parts.

Firstly, there is the introduction, which runs from the beginning of the first book as far as this part of the fifth. Then there is the actual discussion of the laws, initially of the laws that relate particularly to the State and the magistrates, and then of those concerning the individual actions of the citizens.

You will no doubt remember that individual laws have their own introductions. At first, the lawgiver is to take the utmost care in selecting the least defiled of the husbandmen and in separating the shepherds who are pure in their ways from those who are not.

He is also to examine the State, and unless compelled by dire necessity he should not inflict violence. He should ensure that wealth is distributed evenly, as far as is possible, so that no men are very rich while others are in need. He should take care that no one amasses wealth unjustly. Rather than create a State full of splendour, he should take pains to create a State where justice abounds.

He should proclaim that truth above all else should be honoured among men and gods. He should promote hospitality towards strangers and a gentle response towards suppliants. He should advise everyone that the soul is commonly deceived and ruined by self-love. He should take measures to ensure that no one who is rich suffers his neighbour to go hungry.

If possible, he should locate the city in the middle of a region where all resources are accessible. He should divide the city into twelve parts and do the same with the entire region. But why twelve parts? That you may understand that such a vast and laborious undertaking needs the help of the whole universe, which is arranged in twelve spheres. The administration of the State should also be in the image of the heavenly kingdom.

Now the celestial State is arranged in twelve signs, like the twelve tribes. And it is not against his interests to entrust his State to twelve gods, since twelve gods are said to preside over the twelve signs of the heavens: to be precise, six gods and six goddesses: Juno, Vesta, Minerva, Ceres, Diana, and Venus; Mars, Mercury, Jupiter, Neptune, Vulcan, and Apollo.

Let some individual entities preside over others: the signs over our limbs, and the gods over the signs. Thus we have Pallas over Aries and our head; Venus over Taurus and our neck; Apollo over Gemini and man's arms; Mercury over Cancer and the chest; Jupiter over Leo and the shoulders; Ceres over Virgo and the belly; Vulcan over Libra and, to speak frankly, the buttocks; Mars over Scorpio and the genitalia; Diana over Sagittarius and the thighs; Vesta over Capricorn and the knees; Juno over Aquarius and the shins; Neptune over Pisces and the feet.

Understand by this that the whole State must be a single unit, though composed of many citizens, just as the body is a unit, though composed of many limbs. Some deities are said to be masculine and others feminine so that you may realise that some things are directed by the deities towards matter and passivity, while others are directed towards forms and actions.

But why does Plato dedicate a particular stronghold of the city to Vesta, Jupiter, and Pallas? Understand that within the divine there are the three sources of all things: Vesta is the source of being, Jupiter of living, and Minerva of understanding. It is in these three that help is to be entreated from the gods.

But when Plato recommends a partitioning of dwellings and fields into five thousand and forty, he is indicating that this number contains many compatible factors. This will be demonstrated in what soon follows, and it can be understood by even a modest arithmetician.

When he discusses the life shared by all the citizens, you will note his wonderful teaching about love and charity, such as we find in the Gospels, and his teaching that one's country is to be cherished above one's mother. If he says that one's country is an immortal goddess, just imagine what he says about the divine soul of the earthly globe, or about the patron deity of one's country, or about the heavenly country!

The Theme of the
Sixth Book of the *Laws*

THERE ARE THREE kinds of causes whereby the different abilities of men manifest in different places. These three kinds are briefly described by Plato at the end of the preceding book. But I think that on this subject it would be profitable to make some link between Book Five and Book Six.

Therefore, let there be, particularly at a decisive time, a cause that produces better men and worse men. Now this cause may be human, natural, or divine. The human cause is a difference in law, upbringing, and custom. The natural cause is a difference in the elements and in food. The divine cause, if I may call upon divine heaven, is the power of the stars and the divinities; for Plato shows that just as different realms of the heavens are ruled by different stars and gods, that is, by the higher angels, so different regions of the earth are also governed by different daemons and the lower angels. Moreover, in the view of astronomers, regions of the earth reflect regions of the heavens, and cities reflect the rising signs.

At this point I do no more than mention the great differences in ability which a difference of daemons causes among the family members of any one man.

Yet we cannot deny that the powers of the higher spirits influence our spirits in some way or another, when we clearly see our bodies being moved by the higher bodies and being constantly changed, in this way or that way, by the air. But the suffering of human bodies is said to be inflicted either by those spirits or by the higher bodies: it spreads in the soul to the extent that the soul, by an acquired or natural disposition, immerses itself in the body.

Now this has some importance, because those bodies move our souls by means of our bodies; but spirits move our souls by means of our bodies and by means of our souls, and also by means of that spirit which physicians often call the link between soul and body. Remember, however, that all the power and the movement that reach us from the gods above always lead to the good by their very nature, since celestial influences always lead to the good.

However, you should not now blame Saturn for the somewhat unbending moroseness and parsimony of human beings; or blame Mars for their foolhardiness and ferocity; or Mercury for their deceitful malice; or Venus for their lustful love-affairs. But what if the gravity of Saturn within us were transformed into the vice of severity by the vices of our own nature, nutrition, and upbringing? What if, in the same way, the magnanimity of Mars were transformed into that form of presumptuousness which is somewhat akin to magnanimity? Or the diligence of Mercury into malice? Or the love of Venus into lust?

Is it not the case that in the Sun's rays, which by their very nature are productive of sight and life, some lose their sight every day, and others their life? And those rays which provide a healthy warmth in the open air, do they not burn in hollow places? But just as the beneficent influence of the rays harms a part, but not the whole, on account of the lower nature, so from the powers of the stars, which are by nature good, and from the excellent gifts of the deities a defect in body or mind may at times arise through a defect in the lower nature or in custom. Yet in the whole there is no defect or evil, just as, in harmony, the second and the seventh notes, which sound dissonant in isolation, sound harmonious when united with all the other parts of the whole.

The followers of Plato sometimes call the lowest daemons evil, since through their duty, as they describe it, they entice us to the lowest good, that of physical reproduction; and to distract us from the highest good to the lowest is rightly judged to be evil in comparison with the highest.

I merely mention for the present the statements that the highest daemons lead us to the good of contemplation, the central ones to the good of action, and the lowest ones to the good of desire; and that we are able to use or abuse all of these: good things happen when we use them, and bad things when we abuse them.

Plato describes the daemons and the gods as natives of the land, not because they are born in the land, but because they protect with special care those citizens who are born there. He further says that a happy State is nurtured by the gods and by the children of the gods, partly meaning that the celestial Jerusalem is inhabited by angels and pure souls, and partly meaning that the happy life of those who, as he says in the *Phaedo*, inhabit the most sacred parts of the earth, is blessed by fellowship with the deities.

After this, Plato moves on in the Sixth Book to the appointment of magistrates: how many are required, how they are elected, and what the function of each magistrate is. Now he says that care over their appointment is so important that having good laws without good magistrates will be not only useless to a State but extremely harmful. It is essential, he says, that those who are going to appoint the magistrates and those who are going to be appointed should be wholly honourable from their youth up, born of the most upright stock, and fully versed in the ways of their fellow citizens.

You will perceive here the astonishingly sound judgement of Plato in the arrangement of the magistrates and their functions in matters both profane and sacred, in war and in peace, in town and in the country. And you will acknowledge and approve of the rule of the aristocrats, which has elements of a monarchy and elements of a democracy and has a constitution somewhere between the two.

You will note that in the allotting of civil offices an equality is always to be maintained: not an arithmetical equality, by which things of like number, measure, and weight are granted to individuals, an equality which is frequently most unjust, but a geometrical equality, by which the deserts of each can be weighed, and functions can be allotted to individuals in such a way that the ratio of deserving to deserts is the same as that of officials to offices; the offices will not match the officials, but will match the meritorious.

You will thus consider the double equality of official to office and of office to the meritorious, and you will judge the former equality to be harmful, and to be useful only if it occurs through lot. But you will judge the latter equality to be always necessary, an equality in which the whole principle of justice resides; and you will conclude that this equality is based on the judgement of Jupiter and that its conception has been transmitted to only a few men; but however much of it is accessible to us, it is through this alone that all things are preserved.

And it is right to attribute the work of this equality to the judgement of the supreme Judge, who, being the only one to penetrate the inner recesses of all and thus the only one to be perfectly cognisant of merits, is assuredly the only one who is fully competent to render to all their just rewards. And he does this in such a way – firstly in heaven and then in the creation – that all things come into being and are maintained solely by such a distribution, which is made according to the nature of each thing. This is confirmed by the ancients and verified in *Gorgias*.

But in the midst of all this, Plato, with his dedication to the training of children, very characteristically re-creates a magistrate specifically for this purpose and wishes him to be considered the most outstanding of all the supreme magistrates in the State, judging that without the wisdom to cultivate the seed in childhood the whole care of the State would be futile.

You will notice at this point that if human nature is well cultivated it becomes full of gentle and divine qualities; and if not, the converse is true. But why does he say that human nature can become fiercer than that of wild beasts? It is because that which has the greatest force for good can also have the greatest force for evil. Again, when the best is turned to its opposite through depravity, it becomes the worst. This matter is discussed in the *Republic*.

Furthermore, ferocity in a depraved man is augmented by the machinations of a penetrating mind inclined to evil. It is also the case that the keenness of human spirits in anger is changed into rage, and that the wrath of certain daemons, as Plato indicates in his letter to the Syracusans and as Homer often observes from the opinions of the Egyptians, draws heroes away from the gods, or daemons, and incites them to fury and bloodshed.

He once more recommends the number five thousand and forty as the most convenient of all in the distribution of magistrates, dwellings, and fields, for this number may be divided into many whole parts. If you divide this number into two halves, each part will, of course, contain two thousand five hundred and twenty; if you divide it into three, each third will be one thousand six hundred and eighty; if into four, each fourth will be one thousand two hundred and sixty; if into five, each fifth will be one thousand and eight; if into six, each sixth will be eight hundred and forty; if into seven, each seventh will be seven hundred and twenty; if into eight, each eighth will be six hundred and thirty; if into nine, each ninth will be five hundred and sixty; if into ten, each tenth will be five hundred and four; but if into eleven, each eleventh will be four hundred and fifty-eight, with a remainder of two elevenths; and if into twelve, each twelfth will be four hundred and twenty. Let us pause here.

But since the number sixty comes to our mind, you will see that if you divide that whole number by sixty, each sixtieth part will be eighty-four; and conversely, if you divide it by eighty-four, each part will be sixty.

It can be seen, however, that Plato emphasises the fact that that number may be divided by twelve to give four hundred and twenty, which, if divided again by twelve, gives thirty-five. If thirty-five is divided by twelve, it gives two, with a remainder of eleven twelfths. But four hundred and twenty is the product of twenty and twenty-one, for twenty, when repeated twenty-one times, becomes four hundred and twenty.

He commends the number twelve and that universal number which is fully adapted to the number twelve, so that, according to him, there are twelve spheres of the world, twelve signs in the Zodiac, and twelve parts in the elements, for each of the four elements is divided into three sections – highest, lowest, and intermediate – which differ in respect of both position and power.

Another grouping of the twelve arises from the elements to include the four substances of the elements and their eight qualities. Four of these qualities are male: heat and cold, lightness and heaviness. Since the first two are alternating principles, there follow two principles of movement with respect to place. Now there are four female qualities, which are more subject to emotion: wetness and dryness, rarefaction and density. Iamblichus declares that these are included in the mysteries of the Egyptians.

Furthermore, it is on the basis of twelve months that the Sun, lord of the planets, pursues his proper course and produces diverse effects.

Lastly, Plato intends each and every part of the State to be thought of as consecrated to God: in fact, to the twelve gods who are the souls of the twelve spheres; to the gods who rule the twelve signs of the Zodiac; and to the twelve orders of the daemons who follow the celestial signs.

But when he says that the twelve parts of the city follow the revolution of the universe, perhaps he also means the full revolution of the eighth sphere, which takes thirty-six thousand years to complete. Thus you may see in the first period of twelve thousand years, according to the ancients, the youthful period of the whole world; in the second, the mature period; and in the third, the period of old age. But these matters are dealt with more appropriately in the *Timaeus*.

Relevant here is what he says in the *Phaedrus*: that the army of gods and daemons is ordered in twelve ranks under Jupiter, their leader. His conclusion at this point is that, partly through the number twelve that is assigned to the tribes and the sanctuaries, and partly through the divine worship that is solemnly renewed twice every twelve months, the parts of the State are prepared for the service of God, so that they are governed by the gods themselves, who are, as it were, firmly established. But he intends the principal public ceremonies to be held twice in order to meet the requirements of the number twelve when applied to the tribes, to the rest of the State, and to the land.

And when he directs sacrifices to be made to the gods and to the children of the gods, he intends the gods to be understood as the souls of the spheres, and their children as the purer daemons. But he directs all these things to be done for the sake of Jupiter, the sole prince of all.

And we should not let what follows pass by in silence: the twelves which we have referred to as pertaining to the whole are represented, as it were, by the twelve that are specific to each man and are seen to consist of the four bodily humours, the four sense-disturbances, and the four virtues.

After the rites to the gods he comes to the rites of marriage, where you will consider the marriage laws and ceremonies, the exhortation to marriage, the duties of husband and wife towards each other and also in respect of the conceiving and upbringing of children.

You will note first and foremost that it is not proper to give care to the procreation of children while in a state of drunkenness or any other mental disturbance, and that through such shortcomings children are born daily who are sickly in both mind and body. You will also commit to memory his secret words: 'May the principle and divinity that is implanted in men preserve all things, if it is bestowed with fitting honour by all who employ its gifts.'

What, then, is the principle, what is the divinity, which is implanted or inherent? The principle, the idea, is the principle of the human design. The divinity is the personal daemon, and also the chief daemon of generation, often known as Lucina.

But why do we say 'implanted' or 'inherent' or 'abiding in'? That you may understand that the divinity is not merely present but is also constantly within, keeping careful watch. It grants particular favour, and thus particular protection, if it is gratefully honoured by those who employ its gift.

After the reciprocal duties of husband and wife, Plato moves to the reciprocal duties of master and servant. Then, by a typical artifice, he returns to the city walls, temples, and palaces, which he says should have been dealt with before marriage.

Here you will note first of all that the courts of the judges and the palaces of the magistrates are positioned very close to the temple, so that human judges may always remember that while they are judging men they themselves are being judged by God; and that they may also remember that the guardians of the city are unable to guard unless God guard the city, and that nothing in the State, not even the smallest detail, should lack a definite order, for if something lacks order it will put what is ordered into disorder.

Most importantly, women's affairs should not lack order and continuous care, for if they are neglected twice as much harm, indeed more than twice as much harm, comes to the State than is the case if men's affairs are neglected.

Together with these subjects, the age of the world is re-considered, for it is said that the beginning of its birth preceded us by an incalculable length of time, which means, if you heed what Moses says, by an incalculable number of days and hours.

Let us end this book with a resolve never to give free rein to the threefold impulse to indulge in food, drink, and intercourse, but to restrain it with the three bridles of fear, law, and true reason, as well as the moderate employment of honourable sports from our childhood onwards, so that through honourable means of relief we may be recalled from what is base and be encouraged, step by step, to follow serious pursuits.

The Theme of the
Seventh Book of the *Laws*

IN THE SEVENTH BOOK Plato returns or, rather, goes forward, with unparalleled care, to the first rudiments of early childhood. Indeed, it might be said that he never digresses from these, judging that all the good and all the evil of the State resides in the good and evil ways of private individuals and that such ways reside in the good and evil training received in the period of earliest childhood. And this he shows with particular emphasis in the first books, and again in the seventh.

On both occasions he is the most punctilious of artists, shading in one place and adding colour in another. In the first books he wishes this kind of carefulness to be considered as the introduction to laws, and in the seventh book he rightly wishes the form to be considered as the earlier substance of laws. For the written laws, he says, will be ineffectual unless preceded by such carefulness. In both places, moreover, he proceeds from the training of childhood to that of youth, and then to that of manhood.

After some laws about religious worship in the earlier books he hastens forward, not inappropriately, to marriage laws, in order to set the origin of the divine being in a sacred context. But after marriage matters he quickly prepares himself for the shaping of children, not simply when they have been born, but also while they are being born, and even before they are born.

In this cultivation of the human seed he is as prudent, as far-sighted, and as careful as is a farmer with the seeds of his crops. But what do you think he has in mind when he says that dealing with the woman's situation is much more critical than dealing with the man's? And that women should abstain from wine on the night when children are going to be conceived? And, indeed, that in the time immediately prior to conception, and for a whole year after conception, they should be free from all mental disturbances?

There is no doubt that these provisions are to ensure that nothing is neglected that applies to the most precise care needed for the cultivation of a human being. But you will notice from these words that Plato considered that both the woman and the man act as the cause in the generation of children. Although Aristotle expressed some dis-

113

agreement with this view, it was accepted by the majority of the best doctors.

Of course, if everyone loves what he produces, and therefore the father loves his son more than his son loves him, and the mother loves her child more warmly than the father does, one may suppose her, together with the man, to be the effective cause of this product. This supposition can also be confirmed by the fact that children resemble their mothers as much as their fathers, and often more so. This personal and commonly occurring resemblance shows that the embryo receives its substance from the work of both father and mother; for every impulse emanating from a cause is channelled to produce a similar effect.

Finally, since there are male and female of the same species, their powers are based on the same principle. They both, therefore, play their part in completing a form on the same principle, which, though it may not be equal on both sides, is at least similar. Yet these matters have little relevance to the laws.

He then touches here on the not inconsiderable question of black bile, a blemish which makes children fearful, difficult, and querulous. Of this humour and its cure we have given a detailed account in the book *On caring for the health of scholars*. But what is relevant to the present context is to know that the existence of the melancholic humour in children does not arise from copulation itself, which is somewhat sanguine and mainly airy, but from some traces of the mother's menstrual blood which have putrefied in the child and have subsequently been converted into black bile through inflammation.

Also responsible for childhood fears is the strange nature of things, so that sounds, such as thunder, and sights, such as masks and lightning-flashes, can inspire terror. A further factor is that reason, as yet unawakened, does not distinguish images from real things: it abandons the soul to the power of the imagination and to arbitrary impulses.

In this state of fearfulness young children are always suffering and always complaining. The situation is exacerbated by the fact that young children are very easily hurt, even by those who are looking after them, and they are troubled by the air and disturbed and disquieted by the violent movement of nature, especially at the beginning of any difficulty.

And so, in the treatment of young children and youths, he recommends the almost continuous use of rhythmical movement, for eight reasons: firstly, because the movements of the child are maintained by movement; secondly, because this measured movement of life enables us to resist the unmeasured agitation created within us by nature and created outside us by the air; thirdly, because movement arouses a natural warmth and thus enlivens the whole body; fourthly, it digests and assimilates food through all the parts of the body; fifthly, it separates off the unwanted excreta; sixthly, it opens blockages and balances the humours; seventhly, it promotes growth; eighthly, it makes the limbs fit and firm.

But we should harmonise the movement, not only through some measure of equality but also through numerical proportion. In many of our letters we have made many statements about the power of music. For the present, it should be enough to understand that if the mind is often pulled in opposite directions by the power of music – first to pleasure and then to sorrow – it is very possible for it to be frequently brought back, from both of these extremes, to a condition midway between these two. And if the mind is called back to stillness from the movement of the body and, conversely, is called forth from stillness to movement, there is no doubt that, by certain musical rhythms, it can be skilfully brought from the movement of succession to an ordered arrangement, and hence, given time, to a steady condition.

Both here and in his second letter to Dionysius, Plato says that this condition is proper to God and gives the greatest protection to human life. But whether pleasure and pain consist in some kind of movement, and how they are defined, are questions which we discuss at greater length in our book *On Pleasure* and in our commentaries on the *Philebus*.

It will be enough for the present if we conclude as follows: The pleasures of taste and touch seem to originate in a return to the natural disposition of the body; pains, on the other hand, seem to occur in a movement away from the natural disposition, when qualities weaken or strengthen, move or come to rest, or change in some other way. Then again, the pleasures of smell, hearing, and sight seem to originate in a return to sensory orderliness, from which we are occasionally distracted by numerous occurrences. Next, the pleasure of imagining seems to lie likewise in a return to an imaging orderliness which is debarred by agitation.

Order which is both imaging and sensory is based on a particular balance of the vital energies, and whenever anything with a similar balance is directed towards it, pleasure arises from the mutual exchange of the senses and the imagination with those things which flow in from the harmonious relationship.

Then the delight of reason originates in a kind of new formation, whereby reason, which would have become formless, or at least deformed, through bodily agitation, is formed in accordance with its own nature and is formed anew.

Finally, the joy of the mind is accomplished through a new formation, whereby the time comes when, by some insight of the intellect, it is re-fashioned into the Idea from which it has fallen on account of the turmoil of a busy life.

If you consider this process in the right way, you will see that human pleasure, to put it briefly, occurs through a return to the natural condition, and that it occurs and is chosen for the sake of this condition rather than for the sake of the return itself. If, therefore, such a condition can be brought about, it should always be chosen as the most steadfast of all things.

But to anyone who thinks about the matter, why does delight in everlasting movement seem preferable to that everlasting stillness? It is because we are deceived by the imagination and belief of the soul, which is joined to the inconstant body and which, through this association, yearns for fickle pleasure, which the soul, once it has been raised above movement, will, of course, reject in favour of the steadfastness of the natural condition.

For the truth is that if we were to have a taste of this natural condition, separated from which we have been placed on earth, just as we have a taste of the movement that turns towards this natural condition, we should certainly esteem the condition itself far above the return movement.

Indeed, just as all the different levels of good things are better when they are within the unchanging principle of the Good than when they are within changeable matter, in the same way the principles of all desirable things are found within reason and the natural condition rather than within changeable matter.

Let this demonstrate that the true joy of God and of things divine resides in a stillness which is incomparably more joyful than all things changeable. Wise people would do well to choose this stillness themselves and then make it available to others, especially to those who are younger. They also have the duty of persuading everyone that pleasure, which arises from movement, is not only short-lived, trivial, and linked with revulsion, but also leads directly to many protracted sufferings of considerable severity.

Now Plato distinguishes two types of rhythmical movement by which we may moderate the inharmonious movements of the early years of life: music and gymnastic. By means of the first we impart order to the spirit and the mind; and by means of the second we impart order to the humours and the limbs.

Within music Plato includes not only songs and musical notes but also poetry and whatever pertains to the orderliness of shapes. Within gymnastic he includes all physical movement in games, sporting contests, and battles. But appreciate that dance is a mixture of the two. He uses all of these as games for carefully training children of all ages, as well as women and men, in the arts of war and peace; and he calls these fundamentals the laws of the country and the bonds of the State. If these supports are removed, the fabric of the State collapses.

Plato ordains that all these principles should be established exactly as if they were fixed by public statutes, for he judges that from troubles of this kind all the troubles in a State eventually arise, and that from the changeable nature of the sports and games and apparatus there follows a change in the laws and the State. You will observe that change, except in evil situations, is the most dangerous of all things, so that even if you make a change for the better you will at some time expose yourself to danger.

Among other things, Plato says that, in the games, sacrifices should be made to the gods, to the children of the gods, and to the daemons: I mean, to the pure daemons, that they may reconcile us to the children of the gods, so that the children of the gods may render the gods propitious to us, and so that, finally, the gods may make us more prepared for the gifts of almighty God.

In this way, of course, just as there is a gradual movement, by body and sight, from one sphere to another, so the primal religion would progress in proper order from the nearer divinities to those further away, giving particular honour in all matters to the one which is closest to the glory of the Highest.

But I am not now speaking of popular superstition or of belief that is merely poetic or even outrageous: I am speaking of the philosophical worship of the gods that was established by the ancient sages as the cognised order of the universe had ordained. This alone is always commended by Plato, who actually laughs at the other two kinds. And when he does make a mere mention of the other two, that is, of gods

117

and the children of the gods, he takes the children to be daemons and heroes: and when he lists the gods, the children of the gods, and the daemons, he takes the gods to be the divinities above the spheres, the children to be the divinities within the spheres, and the daemons to be the divinities below the spheres.

Later, when he gives his approval to the discipline of games, he says that games are to be designed for the sake of studies, rather than studies for the sake of games. He adds that if matters of human concern are compared to matters divine they are not worthy of any attention, that is, they are not worthy of any esteem or love, and they are not to be considered as serious but as trifling. Yet if they are compared to natural things, he agrees that they should be made much of.

Then he says that the best thing to have happened to man is that he has been granted a disposition suited to games and eager to find both solace from the toils of life and discipline through compatible games. But because the soul moves on its course through various forms of life, like a dance-chorus, they think that this is the best for all.

Again, all the souls of nature, that is, as many as lie within her power, are brought forth into the light by some alternating process. But why does he not say that other creatures, too, are the playthings of the gods? It is because they are not so familiar with the gods that they play with them.

They are not compared to the gods, inasmuch as they are not united with God, and divine things are never measured, and so they are obliged, as it were by the gods, to measure us. And, of course, if it is in God's nature to laugh, He will laugh at the human game of attempting to measure the immeasurable.

You will note here that the words of Plato which we have related from dawn until this time seem to me to be not without some inspiration of the gods and to have some similarity with poetry. He means here that all his writings on him while daylight lasts, that is, until old age, were in some way divinely inspired and were presented practically, so that they are, for the most part, to be expounded allegorically.

He also intimates as much immediately after the beginning of the *Phaedrus*, in order that we may know that what he wrote in his youth and in advanced old age is highly redolent of poetry. This is why he says in his *Letters* that his meaning can be understood by no one, or by very few, and even then only after a long time, with difficulty, and with prophetic insight.

At this point, moreover, consider how carefully Plato restrains unbridled childhood; how much he condemns drowsiness but praises wakefulness; how appropriately he arranges the duties suitable for each period of life, directing that games should be interspersed firstly with letters, secondly with music, thirdly with gymnastic, fourthly with arithmetic, fifthly with geometry, sixthly with astronomy, and seventhly with dialectic, that is, with metaphysics; in the last position he puts the study of laws and of the State.

But when he says that God never fights against necessity but fights against human necessity, you should note that the first necessity abides in the natural order of creation, which has been divinely established so that things are of such a kind, of such a number, and of such a measure, and that they act and move in a particular way, with some preceding, some accompanying, some following, some together, and some separate; and as they are, so they are to be judged. The second necessity consists in a falling away from the natural order, a falling away which appears to be deformed, unnatural, incongruous, and disconnected.

God does not fight against the first necessity, for such necessity exists through His specific will. But why does He fight against the second necessity? It is true that there is no place where God fights, for what can stand against the Almighty? Nevertheless, He is imagined as fighting because this necessity, having fallen from the divine likeness, then falls further into a deformity which is very unlike God and is now in opposition to Him, but which is one day miraculously restored to order by God, as if He is fighting back and subduing it.

Notice next a statement of no small significance: Inexperience is not the worst of all things. But experience that is wrongly acquired is the worst of many things. And if you heed the earlier statement, which names man as god, as daemon, and as hero, you will understand how Plato can be expounded when he says that the human soul moves across into different species. But we have spoken more fully of this in the *Theology*.

In the same way, when he encourages young people to study mathematics, he reproaches the Greeks, for they have all lost their way in geometry and astronomy: in geometry, because they have come to think that any measurement is commensurable with any other, something that the barbarians discovered was impossible; and in astronomy, because they said that the planets wander, although there can be no error in things divine. Again, they put the slowest movement among the fastest movements, and they said that the fastest was one of the slowest.

Plato considers that speaking false words against the dignity of the gods through ignorance born of carelessness is more than foolish: it is profane. But his strongest condemnation is reserved for the mistake made by the Greeks in opposition to the will of divine providence, for they say that it is not right to search for God, the maker and source of the world, or for the cause of the things that are in the world, as if such a search had no part in religion, although it is, in fact, the most religious thing of all, for it has a strong affinity with the divine will, which has not only ordered the universe in such a way that there is a constant attraction towards a search of this kind, but has also filled the mind itself with eagerness to make the search.

We have shown elsewhere, and we now confirm by his earlier words in the present work, that Plato himself considered the truest religion to be most strongly established on the worship of the one God; for although he often says that gods (in the plural) are to be worshipped, his final conclusion is that, through a single religion, God Himself (in the singular) is the worthy recipient of all holy devotion.

Moreover, in the earlier parts of the work, when he was going to elect the judges, he gathered all the magistrates together in the temple at the very beginning of the year. But he made the summer solstice the beginning of the year. Let it not trouble you that the solstice is said to be on the calends immediately following the solstice, for this is a more definite beginning in the minds of the people, but the true beginning for the people is at the solstice itself.

This should be expounded allegorically, as follows: When the light of the sun, that is, the light of God, is more rightly and more fully received by us, this is the true beginning of living and thinking and deciding; and for the sake of this One all are gathered together in a single temple, that is, all are practising a single religion, whatever the form of their practice. But in the books of the *Republic* he says that the light of the sun is the image of the Father of all and that it has been placed by the Father of all, as His image, in this earthly temple.

What more is there to say? The one God is to be worshipped first and foremost; the other divinities are to be cultivated for His sake. This is what Plato frequently teaches in different writings and what he clearly demonstrates in his letter to Dionysius and his letter to Hermias; in *Parmenides*, which is all about the One; in the *Timaeus*, which shows how all comes forth from the One; in *Philebus*, which measures all by the One; and in *Epinomis*, which returns everything to the One

The Theme of the
Eighth Book of the *Laws*

THE STATEMENTS which we have just presented from the many made by our Plato concerning the true and unified worship of the one god can also be confirmed beyond peradventure by reference to the *Phaedrus, Gorgias, Protagoras*, the *Statesman, Critias*, and the fourth book of the *Laws*. For in these dialogues he subjects the whole congregation of the gods, if I may call it thus, to a single king, as to one who rules over all, one who makes a just allocation of functions to all and sundry, and one who thus arranges human affairs; not to one who seems to be far away from here but rather, as is clear in the fourth book of the *Laws*, to one who wills it to be so.

Plato therefore directs, first of all, that God should be worshipped for His own sake; that the subsequent divinities, which partake of Him and are also called gods, should be loved for their similarity to Him, honoured as His representatives, summoned as reconcilers, heard as interpreters of the divine mind, and, finally, heeded as heralds of the divine majesty.

Plato directs that temples should be founded in the city, and he divides the city itself into twelve parts, as if it were a holy place, just as God has built, as a temple for Himself, a world that is adorned with the music and dances of the twelve spheres and supplied with priests, that is, with spirits endowed with reason, who praise God in all places and at all times.

Striving as far as possible to imitate that temple made by God, Plato allows many deities into his temples, just as God Himself allows many into His temple; and he arranges many images there, just as God has placed the stars in the firmament as images of His angels.

Furthermore, among the numerous altars of many temples, he consecrates the chief altar first of all, just as from among the stars God has chosen the Sun to be an image peculiar to Himself, as Plato says in the *Republic*; concerning which it may be relevant to say 'He has placed His tabernacle in the Sun'. But sacrifices and statues will be written about more thoroughly elsewhere.

Let me say briefly, for the present, that Plato wishes God to be worshipped by the mind alone, without any material attributes or anything of a similar nature. But he allows animals and other sacrifices to be offered to the subsequent deities, as the law of the country directs.

Hence the theologians of different peoples added many visual items, such as diagrams and lights, to rituals which were in honour of the celestial and fiery divinities. To the rituals in honour of the airy deities they introduced musical harmonies, fragrances, and vapours. In the rites honouring the watery and earthy deities they made use of things relating to taste and to firmness of texture.

This is why no one should be surprised that Plato, a philosopher of such seriousness, never promulgated any of his laws, especially the sacred ones, without consulting the oracles. Initially, it seemed right to make allowances for the times. Indeed, it was necessary to strengthen human affairs with some divine counsel and authority; yet it was impossible for the men who were born at that time and brought up in that way to be held in divine worship on any basis that was alien to their traditions.

Then Plato, in his great wisdom, judged that, although impure spirits could deceive men through oracles, minds that are abstracted from the body through divine worship are at once caught up, as if already pure, by the pure divinities; and just as wood, which the wind has happened to dry out, often bursts into spontaneous fire, so can souls which have performed some religious ritual, even a ritual not strongly approved of by the wise, be caught up in some unknown way by a higher divinity, so that, without knowing how, they rise up beyond the senses and into the mind itself and are now blissfully set ablaze from on high.

Plato considers that less heed should be taken of the ritual with which you worship the divine than of the divinity for whose sake you are undertaking the worship. For if you are undertaking it for the sake of the supreme King of all and with a desire for things eternal and good, it is probable that, whatever your starting-point and your initial practices, you will one day, through such worship, draw closer to the Supreme and be suffused with its boundless light, or at least be protected by its abounding goodness.

This is why Plato, trusting in an assurance of this kind, consults the oracles concerning the establishment of laws and sacrifices and directs one of the magistrates to undertake public worship every day, primarily for the welfare of the country and secondarily for his own welfare and that of his household.

And following a definite sequence, he quickly moves from the basic principles concerning youth, which were communicated in the seventh book, to the holy matters of the eighth book, in the manner of someone who wishes it to be understood that men are properly trained from their earliest years to have the desire and the ability to participate aright in holy observances.

But if some quibbler or timid person is afraid to mingle with so many gods and daemons in the Platonic State, he is equally welcome to go to the Aristotelian city, which is devoid of daemons and gods and even of God Himself. Yet it is certainly worthwhile for someone who is superstitious, haughty, and given to irritability, to select the most powerful things of all, to approve Platonic piety, and not to require that he be a Christian whom nothing but an interval of time has prohibited from being so.

Of holy rites, the first are the twelve which begin the months; the second are the twelve in the middle of the months; and the third are the three hundred and sixty-five daily rites. There are the special rites to the heavenly deities; the intermediate rites to the earthly deities, that is, to the deities that rule beneath the Moon, for all those under heaven he calls earthly; the lower rites to the daemons; and the lowest rites to the heroes.

But he considers it necessary to categorise the rites into twelve kinds altogether, for, in conformity with the twelve spheres and signs, the daemons and heroes are also divided into twelve groups within each sphere. Yet his direction is that the observance of the solemnities and their distinction should be proclaimed to the people in the last month of every year, which by common custom we take as February, but which in the Platonic tradition is the month before the summer solstice.

He rightly dedicates the last month to Pluto, for Pluto is the providence which separates souls and then judges them when they have been separated. But he says that the union of the soul with the body is not better than its separation from the body. You should understand that he is referring to the transient body and its transient nature and not to the celestial body or a body similar to the heavens.

It is good to be united to a celestial body, but not to a transient body. But if being joined to this body also is said to be worthwhile, the statement should be made not on account of the body itself but for the sake of some other end. We have written at greater length on these matters in the *Theology*.

But is it possible that the followers of Plato make offerings to even the impure daemons, to some because they preside over natural functions, and to others lest they cause harm through their ill-will? Yet Plato has in no way countenanced this, especially since he directs rites to be performed only for the purification of the mind and the worship of the first God.

Now he affirms that the State will be happy when it employs laws in accordance with divine counsel. He adds that it is particularly pertinent to the prosperous life of the citizen and of the State neither to inflict harm on others nor to be afflicted by harm; and that both conditions can be achieved through virtue.

To prevent the State from suffering harm, he has ordained sacrifices in which divine assistance is obtained through petition; and solemn games and festivals are held which bear the closest resemblance to war-like battles. His intention is that both women and men should be trained for battle by taking part in these games, and that each person is trained to use the left hand as well as the right. The aim is for the State to be whole, with both sexes equally useful, and for each member to be fully unified, with both hands equally useful.

At this point you will mark his abhorrence of greed, which is particularly harmful to the State because it busies men's minds with their own petty gains and thus diverts them from care for the public welfare. You will also note how cautious he is about allowing music, dancing, and poetry into the sacred war-like games. You will then note that the only rule that is both legitimate and safe is the one in which a willing ruler governs willing subjects.

But since loves – loves of the basest sort – often occur in meetings for youthful games, he warns that very careful measures should be taken to deal with these, although to a large extent he has already implemented such measures by parting the citizens from their gold and silver, by training them in hard toil, and by meticulously subjecting all, and particularly the youth, to the gaze of those who observe their judgements and habits in all places. He considers these three to be specially wholesome remedies for the disease of licentiousness and wantonness.

He also makes provision for the fourth and current remedy, which is that from the students of the laws and from the magistrates a daily report should be disseminated by which all, through common consent, may grow into the habit of thinking that unnatural sexual intercourse is no less wicked than intercourse between children and their parents. But Plato thinks that the unanimity in the general report exerts a wonderful influence on character.

At this point you will hear that the man who overcomes pleasure lives happily, while the man who is overcome by pleasure lives unhappily. You will also hear that most wholesome directive towards abstinence which meets with the fullest approval of the Apostle Paul: that if athletes abstain from pleasures through zeal for physical victory, much more zealously should all abstain for the sake of that victory which pertains to the soul.

Besides, there is a double benefit. The first benefit is generated through similarity of character, and the second through a certain need; and each, when it waxes strong, is called love. Love itself, in this context, is threefold: love for the beauty of the soul alone; love for the body alone; and love for both simultaneously.

In these matters, consider how cautiously he proceeds in introducing laws, so that there are occasions in the dialogues when he has made some allowance for the honourable lover of the physical form, but here he makes no allowances: there is no doubt that he expressly banishes love for the body alone. Yet in the *Laws* he dare not admit the love for body and soul combined, not even in moderation. In the end, he is seen to give his clear approval only to love for the soul alone.

But then he says, and not without justification, that men of depraved nature are not masters of themselves. For there is no doubt that anyone who departs from reason and thus loses the rational nature of man loses his freedom at the same time, for freedom is the gift of reason. Yet he never loses his responsibility, even though he seems to lose the impulse, since he himself has provided the cause for a difficulty of this kind.

But men who are quite different from these, I mean men of unblemished nature, he describes as those who worship God, who fear ill report more than anything else in human affairs, and who do not love the beauty of any body, their own or that of another, but love the beauty of soul and character.

When he said earlier that the work of God was to withstand misdeeds, if they could be regulated by Him, understand him to mean that it is a characteristic of God, the regulator of all natures which have fallen from the natural order, to restore them to order, especially since many hold the view that the soul initially fell into such misfortunes at the prompting of certain daemons rather than at the prompting of the senses. But when he says, 'If they could be regulated by Him,' his doubt is not about divine power but about human power. Of course, God has full power within Himself to regulate, but man cannot be regulated so easily. If He willed to drag someone of necessity, God could compel him, but His will is to lead him without compulsion.

Presently, Plato speaks of the banquets which are interspersed with the sacred rites and the games. Again, with reference to the banquets, he speaks of the relevant food and laws. But at the right moment, after the training of the soul and the relevant laws, he moves on to food for the body and laws of this kind.

Then he states the laws concerning fields, boundaries, water, natural products, flocks, herds, pasture-lands, and such like. But when he is speaking of boundaries and says that anyone who transgresses boundaries is punished by Jupiter, by a fellow tribesman, and by a guest, you should understand that Jupiter is the sole protector of both the fellow tribesman and the guest. And since transgression of the boundaries which are decreed by law and the usurpation of someone else's lordship to oneself is a characteristic of pride, he says that Jupiter is aroused to avenge this wrong and to rise up with battles of the most hostile kind; it is as if he is saying that God rises up against the proud, not so much as a judge as an avenging enemy.

But after enunciating many principles, he says that it is not the task of an older philosopher to spell out precisely some of the minor laws, especially those relating to litigation and controversial matters, but to state a few of the common laws about external matters, laws which the interpreters of the law trace in the minutest detail, and to go through most punctiliously and precisely the laws concerning character and the training of the soul.

But when he speaks of the various craftsmen, he gives three precepts to be thoroughly committed to memory. The first is that no citizen, that is, no one who is at any time going to perform any public functions, should be engaged in any craft, and the same holds true for his slave, since the art of governing a State requires long training and much learning, and thus claims the whole man for itself. The second is that no one should or can practise two arts or pursuits. The third and last is that it is not fitting for one craftsman to exercise control over a craftsman of a different skill.

Plato wisely forbids the export of goods which the citizens need, and the import of anything unnecessary, and above all he forbids trade, especially if it is for the sake of profit.

Then he lays out the twelve parts of the city, with streets and temples and market-places; and to the market-places he assigns laws which are both sensible and scrupulous.

The Theme of the Ninth Book of the *Laws*

AFTER THE GENERAL training of character and the handing down of many laws, the ninth book now addresses legal judgements, and it does so in a way that is both powerful and appropriate: for those who have been trained in matters of character and instructed in the laws can now make judgements, and those who did not submit to earlier training and instruction are now to be judged.

Wisely did our doctor of souls strive until now to give wholesome directions and thus preserve the full health of the soul, but now that it has been lost he is trying hard to restore it. In accordance with Platonic love, he is compelled and, as it were, dragged, through compassion and sorrow, towards excision and cauterisation, yet with such kindly care that he comforts the seriously sick with the most soothing words imaginable and he strives to make them well with words that are like magical songs, before he resorts to his medical skill, which even then he applies in such a way that the sick person is scarcely aware of it, finding in it much more hope than pain, and drawing from the pain health rather than injury.

A man of great mercifulness punishes no one without providing a means of solace. He never hurts anyone who has received a punishment. He does his utmost to save everyone; and those he does not punish he makes it his business to free from the ills of the soul; and he takes it upon himself to resist even the slightest pang of death and the great and ever-growing troubles of the soul.

But he states that it is better to depart from here than to live with incurable illness of soul or body; and yet he deprives no one of life unless he knows him to be incurable, and he does not wish to direct at the trouble any punishment imposed by the law, which is good.

Furthermore, he says that the penalty itself is good, for many reasons: it is just, and justice is good; it washes away a present evil, or prevents a future evil; by punishing a single person, it sets an example and cleanses the State of many ills. And, to speak briefly, he always intermingles justice with mercy in an amazing way, and does not apply the excessive pressure that comes from harshness or leave anything unsatisfied as a result of softness.

But just as he has previously propounded divine duties before human duties, so now he wisely deals with sacrilege before all other offences. And while he shows the serious nature of the offence against the divine majesty, it is under the inspiration of God that he indicates that nothing of the kind has ever before been perpetrated by men as long as some divine grace has flourished within them.

But when that grace has been lost through other offences, men, becoming almost strangers to God, begin to sin against God through sacrilegious offences, so that sacrilege itself is not just a sin but is also a punishment for sin, I mean a punishment which does not cleanse but which destroys. For such a penalty is imposed not by the law but by the transgression of the law.

But when he says that the first lawgivers were the sons of God and that the laws were handed down to the heroes, who had been begotten by the gods, his words are to be expounded by what he says in *Critias* and the *Statesman* and in many other places, with the meaning that the sons of God are to be understood here as the gods beneath the Moon, who are equipped to govern various parts of the Earth respectively. In the Platonic tradition we may also call them angels.

In *Protagoras* he teaches that it is through them, under the name of Mercury, that the human race rightfully received the laws; in *Critias*, too, he says that the first men born from the Earth received the laws, and those men he here names heroes, sprung from the gods, that is, men sprung from the Earth through the work of the gods. In *Critias*, however, he says that those laws were not composed for the physical ears but were passed by some kind of inspiration from the divine minds into human minds, and that, as long as men complied with them, they lived in happiness.

He adds that when men transgressed such laws they lost divine grace; when this was lost, they also lost happiness; being unhappy, they gave vent to their feelings with sacrilegious acts, through which they eventually became very bad and very unhappy. Thus may be understood the mystery of the earthly paradise and man's expulsion from it.

But note that, in his enquiries into the causes of sacrilege, three causes are given for serious offences. The first is the general weakness of the human race, confirmed by custom; the second is daemonic prompting or suggestion; the third is destructive guilt, the indelible mark of ancient unpurged sins, which goads men to commit the most heinous offences. This seems to be very similar to original sin, which many theologians have discussed at great length.

This is why the divine Plato, when addressing the sacrilegious man, says: 'It is neither a human ill nor a divine ill that drives you to sacrilege.' Understand that human ill is human weakness, with its proclivity for lower things, while divine ill is, as they say, diabolical guile. But he does not accept either of these, not because they are not responsible for sacrilege but because they are not its only causes.

For close to these is the third and real cause of sacrilege, which he adds when he says: 'But the fatal prompting is engendered from original, unexpiated sin, by which the soul, no longer human but bestial, undoubtedly commits sacrilege against God, possessing no more the reason of God now that it has lost human reason, the image of divine reason.'

But Plato soon checks the initial prompting to commit sacrilege, as if it were a disease in its early stages, with three remedies to counteract the three causes from which it arises. Firstly, in order to suppress the violent impulse, he directs us to the holy expiations which in the Christian tradition we may name repentance, confession, alms-giving, and fasting.

Secondly, in order to stand firm against devilish intrigues, he directs us to prayers and supplications, by which we may be protected from the lower spirits by the higher and liberating spirits.

Finally, in order that human frailty may be supported, he directs us to shun the company of bad men and adopt the company of good men.

Accordingly, just as he had ordained that after God one's native land was to be worshipped, so after acts of sacrilege, which are perpetrated upon people or things that are consecrated to God, he proceeds to punishable crimes and offences which are committed against one's native land and which he considers very close to acts of sacrilege, including them together and administering a similar punishment.

These offences he deems to be of three kinds, for to sin against one's homeland and to be considered an enemy of one's homeland it is necessary to discount the laws and refer the guiding principle to human will and whim; to refrain, even though one has the power, from aiding one's country when in danger; and, from being a son, to become a traitor to one's country through greed or any other reason.

At this point he re-states the duty of the lawgiver, which he intends to be not that of a master drawing up laws for his servants but that of a father writing laws for his children, a father who persuades as much as he threatens, who teaches as much as he commands, who entices as much as he terrifies.

Thus the task of the lawgiver is not so much the drawing up of commands as the training of character, for its aim is, one way or another, to make the citizens good and happy. But to punish the bad there must be a need, rather than a will, to do so. And because of all human laws only the laws of Plato embrace all these things, they are the most perfect of all human laws and should almost be numbered among the divine laws rather than among the human.

And it is not without significance that the very beginning of this discussion takes its rise from God, with the additional statement from Plato that it seems to him that all these things have been divinely inspired.

Finally, from this discussion there is a straight pathway to the blessed temple of supreme Jove, that is, a pathway to heaven. But since specific levels of punishment are to be prescribed by the lawgiver and recommended by the judge for specific levels of culpability with regard to sacrilege, parricide, and other crimes, he presents a very convenient way of distinguishing these levels: every practice is either virtuous or vicious.

If it is virtuous, it is completely voluntary, for it has been acquired through freedom of judgement, unhampered choice, and the activities of one's own mind and soul. But if it is a vicious practice, it is deemed to be totally involuntary, for the sickness of mind and soul, like the sickness of the body, arises from imbalance of the humours. No one would say that sickness is voluntary, although it may be said that some things which undoubtedly lead to disease are in some measure voluntary. Furthermore, this kind of practice develops from hampered judgement, from stressful choice, and from passion, rather than from actions.

From these considerations comes that statement of Plato which has been so often repeated: Vicious practices are involuntary; no one commits evil voluntarily, just as no one willingly becomes ill, deformed, or impoverished.

After distinguishing practices, he goes on to distinguish actions. Actions tend to give rise to the practice of virtue or the practice of vice. In the case of the former, they are so completely voluntary that the practice is said to be voluntary. In the latter case, they are said to be partly voluntary, because they occur with some degree of consent from the mind and because they could not occur before they actually occurred; and they are said to be partly involuntary, because they lead a person unwittingly towards harm, degradation, and sickness, which no one wants, and because they arise from ignorance of the end or outcome. Inasmuch as they occur through ignorance they are considered to occur outside the will of reason.

The distinction is this: human actions, as far as the substance of the laws and judgements is concerned, are grouped into five categories: those which spring forth from strong feelings of desire; those which burst forth under the impulse of the wrathful nature; those which arise from simple ignorance which causes the person to be ignorant of the situation, although no one can be ignorant of himself; those which occur through a double ignorance, by which the person is ignorant of the situation and, at the same time, of his own ignorance, while thinking that he knows; and, finally, those actions which arise from some reasonable viewpoint, I mean, a viewpoint based on reason and on the laws concerning what is just and what is unjust.

After making this distinction, he next distinguishes the rules of judgement by which those who offend through desire are dealt with in one way, while those who offend through anger are dealt with in another way; a further distinction is made between those who have offended intentionally and those who have offended unintentionally; and, again, consideration is given as to whether the offence was forceful and open or furtive and deceptive.

Next, can it be said that the error occurs through ignorance, either simple ignorance or twofold ignorance? But when, in dealing with the judgements of homicides, he brings forward the problem of those who are slain whilst taking vengeance on killers, take note that, in Plato's view, the disturbances which are related to the sensory world can persist in the soul which is separated from this body, for in Plato's view some primal sensory nature endures, the real origin of all the other senses, and through this the soul within this body expands the powers of sensing into these instruments, and when it leaves the body it unfolds the same powers upon itself, or rather, to speak more in keeping with the manner of Plato, it exercises these powers in an airy body. Being enveloped by the airy body, it enters it and it also comes forth from it.

Concerning these matters, the followers of Plato draw this distinction: the soul dwells but a short time in this coarse body, but in the airy body it dwells many ages, and in the celestial body it dwells for all time.

What is all this leading to? The point is that you should not be surprised that disturbances continue to exist in the soul of a dead person, if the sense impressions and memories of these things persist. But the theologians of old thought it likely that the souls of men who meet a sudden death, being unpurified, are troubled by disturbances, and that they also stir up their enemies, not only through human resentment but also through divine retribution and the spirit of foresight.

Our Virgil, a follower of Plato, gives evidence that, in the view of the ancients, there remained in the soul a sense and a passion for retribution which made use of the airy body. For what else does he intend by the words, 'And now my great image will go to the regions below the earth'? Exactly as Plato would do, he calls the primal nature of perception the image of the rational soul. But why 'great'? Because it is the origin of the other senses, and it is the common sense, and after this body it makes use of the great body, the airy body, which, having made its way inside it, becomes rather confined. When it has been removed, it expands, as the nature of the airy element requires.

And again, 'As a shade I shall be present in all places, and thou wilt pay the penalty unreasonably.' He draws a distinction between 'image' and 'shade': he takes 'image' to be the perception of the soul within the airy body, and the airy body itself to be the 'shade' of the soul. But the dark earthy body he calls a prison.

And what he says on the judgements relating to homicide (especially parricide) and the return of the human soul to human bodies, in which it frequently pays a penalty that corresponds to the blame incurred in a previous life, expresses the ancient view of the Magi and the Egyptian priests. For they judged that there was nothing more suited to the purging away of human shortcomings than for souls, at some point in time, to suffer in human bodies what they themselves had committed.

This is the principle used by Plotinus of Egypt, in his books on Providence, to resolve points of uncertainty which are regularly raised against divine providence and justice. For he says that whatever is not repaid through divine providence in this life is repaid in full in another life, another human life. He says that it is also repaid even in the beasts, when the soul that was once human becomes the soul of a beast. But he seems to have been the only one to hold this last view. For the other followers of Plato rejected the suggestion that the soul that is proper to a man could ever become proper to a beast.

However, they do agree, on the other hand, that the soul takes up a new abode in other human beings, something that Plato is not definite about, although he considers it very likely. He often reviews the idea that it passes into beasts, but in giving particular attention to the point he sets aside his customary seriousness and speaks humorously, in order to show beyond doubt that the idea should be refuted and that it should be seen as an allegory.

Thus you may take the movement into beasts in two ways: firstly, as a movement into an emotional state, an imagining, a way of life fit for a beast; and secondly, as a movement into dwelling and associating with beasts for an allotted time, as a punishment, for the ancients consider that the company and characteristics of beasts constitute nothing more than a punishment, while a return to the human condition, where identical or similar things are experienced, is not only a punishment but is also a process of purification.

Happening by good fortune to refer next to the necessity of the law, he affirms that law is necessary for the human race; for without laws the human race would be in no whit distinguishable from the most abominable beasts. In adducing the cause for this, he says that no man's natural powers are able to form a clear understanding of all that needs to be understood to promote the public good; and if he did happen to know this, he would not always have the power or the will to enact what he knew.

Now if, by some divine grace, there were to arise within humanity some soul which understood the public good in all respects and made that his noble purpose at all times, there would, for that time, be no need for any laws, either for that person or for his country; for a mind that is true and free transcends all laws and will rightfully rule over all. But since no one like this has been found, he concludes that we must necessarily live under laws.

He says, too, that self-interest causes deep divisions within the State, whereas zeal for the public good unites; that a destructive plague holds sway over that State in which judgement from the magistrates is either silent or full of noise and shouting.

And if his statement that a congenial daemon frequently offers resistance to many evils makes you shudder at the word 'daemon', then you may use the name 'angel', with Plato's agreement, or you may remember that our 'daemon' and 'genius' is not only our intellect, as some believe, but a divinity, too.

His next direction is that older people should be so deeply honoured with the respect due to parents that, even when beaten by them, you are not to be angry but must bear it patiently.

Yet, following the astronomical tradition, we should accept our natal planets, which he here calls gods, not the ascending signs and the lords of the signs, but the Idea, the principle, of the human race and the guardian angel of our life.

Finally, he warns us to beware of the wrath of the gods and the punishment inflicted by the infernal spirits. He warns us that death is not the final punishment, but that beyond this there are the torments meted out by the devils, and he declares that these things have been stated with the utmost truth in all respects.

The Theme of the
Tenth Book of the *Laws*

THE BEGINNING of the tenth book expands on the last part of the ninth, reminding us that judgements concerning force inflicted upon an object are to be made subsequently to the judgements, as laid down in the ninth book, concerning force inflicted upon the person. But since no force is harsher or harder to bear than that which is inflicted with a degree of contempt, it is not surprising that, in his judgement, affronts and injustices born of contempt, whether perpetrated against the person or the possession, are to be sorted out into their respective groupings, of which there are, in fact, five.

For the offences may be committed against public worship, private worship, or the respect due to parents; or they may be against the high status of the magistracy or the noble civic dignity of some citizen. He therefore entrusts these matters, for the most punctilious judgement, to all the other authorities of law in addition to the magistrates and judges.

Then he distinguishes from all others those offences which are committed in contempt of the gods, as if such offences are, more than words can express, the most serious of all. The whole focus of the tenth book is on such offences.

But he first indicates what difference lies between sacrilege and impiety. Sacrilege he describes as a forcible carrying off of a thing or person dedicated to the gods: an action that is included as a type within the broader category of impiety. For apart from sacrilege there are included within impiety many other offences in contempt of the gods: offences in thought, word, or deed; offences of commission, permission, and omission.

And lest anything should escape our attention, it is made clear that impiety also includes every relationship and association begun at meals or in conversations with those who, through unavoidable misfortunes, are kept away from what is holy and who, being corrupt, corrupt others too, even by their presence. At the end of the ninth book he examines this subject in such a way that he seems to have anticipated the imprecations uttered by our people to drive the profane away from the communion of the Church.

So then our doctor, wishing to give a really thorough purification to souls weakened by the disease of impiety, begins by pursuing the causes of this disease. And while he is searching, he communicates the message of the Gospel, for he says: 'Whoever believes in God according to the laws is religious and never does or says anything profane.' How right he is to have shown here that the starting-point is faith! A faith that is to be applied to the laws!

But someone who is not troubled by the number of angels should not, I hope, be troubled by the number of gods. For in Plato's view the number of gods does not exceed the number of angels and blessed spirits in which we believe.

What, moreover, do the laws – the laws which are sacred and the oldest of all the laws — say of God and of the angels who serve God?

They say three things. The first is that these are gods. The second is that they provide for all. The third is that they justly weigh rewards and punishments against what is deserved. The whole of religion is founded on the trustworthiness and observance of this judgement.

Who, then, is irreligious? Clearly, the man who denies that such gods exist; or, if they do exist, that they provide; or, even if they do provide, that they give a just balance: which is tantamount to thinking that the gods, in the manner of human judges, can be easily appeased merely by gifts, even by gifts offered by an unjust man.

Plato, therefore, wishing to remove the three causes of the disease of irreligion, will prove that the gods exist: those that are within the world as rulers of the spheres of the world, and those that are above the world as contemplators of almighty God. He will demonstrate that the gods provide for all, even for the least, and that with the unerring balance and scale of rightful justice it is not the outward offerings of the hands that are weighed, but the innermost merits of men's souls.

Finally, through this teaching, as if through some prologue to the law, he will deter everyone from all contempt of the gods and urge everyone to practise piety. He will also terrify and torment the wicked with the threats and whips of the laws.

To begin with, he shows through two general lines of reasoning that the gods exist. His first argument is derived from the universal nature of creation, and the second is derived from the human race. The first argument is as follows: We have ascertained that in all places order proceeds from reason; that at no time and in no place is order interrupted by the power of reason; and that order is rendered most beneficial by reason at its finest level. Since, therefore, the arrangement of the whole creation is a highly ordered progression at all times and in all places, and does not lack a wonderful appropriateness, it follows that the world is necessarily arranged and moved by the highest and most powerful level of reason.

And since the universe is one, and one cannot be made from diverse elements except by one, it follows that this supreme reason is one and that a number of divine reasons or principles exist beneath the supreme divine reason or principle, just as in a single universal operation that is ordered in accordance with reason there are many spheres that differ from one another in type and in power; and they are all so completely ordered in accordance with reason that the worlds, which are many from one point of view, seem to be contained within the vast embrace of a single world.

And so, in the same way, the numerous rulers of apparently constricted worlds, being then put into order, are included in the single ruler of a world that is infinitely vast. In fact, this ruler himself is, if I may say so, limitless order, rejoicing much more in the regulator than in what is regulated. In this respect, if he is delighted, as he indubitably is, by the multitude of things that are ordered within the creation, he is also highly pleased by the numerous regulators, for the outstanding greatness of the greatest king lies in the fact that he has beneath him many great kings in addition to minor vassals.

Now the second relevant line of reasoning, drawn from the human race, is as follows: The natural prompting of any species cannot be pointless, and the natural judgement of the finest species of living creatures cannot be entirely false. But since the human race, the finest species of living creatures, is in all respects, in all places, and at all times guided to religion by a natural prompting and unvarying judgement, it follows of necessity that there are gods who are worshipped through religion and that souls survive the death of bodies; and this is the unshakeable foundation of religion. Give heed to the words of Plato: The principles concerning divine matters, even if they are at times not expressed very eloquently, are nevertheless true.

Again, he says that there are two circumstances conducive to irreligion: intemperance, which is the strong desire for physical pleasures, and the ignorance that is born of the ridiculous views of certain poets and natural philosophers. He says that poets have made three errors with respect to the gods. Firstly, they proclaim that the gods have sprung forth from the confusion which they call Chaos. Secondly, they declare that the gods are born from various parents and conceived in a way similar to human intercourse. Thirdly, through wicked irreligion, they attribute all human agitations, errors, and outrages to the gods.

He says, too, that those natural philosophers have offended against religion who, with Democritus, dream that the universe, with its wondrous order, is arranged by blind chance rather than by divine principle, or who, with Anaxagoras and Archelaus, hold that the heavens contain nothing more divine than the elements. They also say that the forms of those things which are created, being clearly directed universally towards some end, arise from an elemental impulse rather than from the skill of a mind which directs each and every thing towards a specific end. But since, in the books of our *Theology* we have expatiated on our refutation of these opinions and on our confirmation of those which we have just proved and which we shall re-state in this digest based on Plato's views, we shall, for the present, deal briefly with this subject.

Consider the great scope of our Plato's religion: how he has shown that God exists, and how, in his disputes with those who deny God, he has scarcely been able to keep himself from anger, a man who in all other respects surpasses everyone in the mildness he displays both in his life and in debates. He certainly emphasises here that those who deny God are not to be tolerated.

Take note that Plato demonstrates that those who offer worship at sunrise and sunset are not really worshipping the Sun and the Moon, but are worshipping the beneficence of God, to whom he bids us give daily thanks for the immeasurable gift of light. He considers a man to be more like a monster if, in spite of his natural instinct, upbringing, and tradition, he denies that the gods exist. But a little later he urges the young men, in case ridiculous views against God have fallen upon their ears, to refrain from making judgements about matters divine and to trust their elders and the laws, until they have learnt from age, experience, and reason.

He goes on to consider the opinions of some people who are held to be wise: opinions which promptly cause men to decline towards irreligion and injustice; opinions, I say, which maintain that the natures of the four elements, flowing together through chance movement, gather everything into a heap, and that religion and justice depend not on truth but on the opinion of men.

This is why he concludes that, in private as well as in public, these most harmful of all things should be refuted by principles and that men should be compelled to heed and obey the laws, not simply by threats and tortures but by persuasion, too, and by principles.

He says that as a general rule man, being a rational creature and therefore free, should not and cannot be bound by anything except the chain of reason. Reason, therefore, should be aroused by the laws, for reason is so powerful in discovering God that after a rational enquiry a man becomes convinced that reason abides more within nature than within himself, and all the more so because he observes that natural operations display more order than human ones do.

From this he observes that, since the skill governing natural activities is more accomplished than man's and also partakes of life and intelligence, it is assuredly alive and intelligent: indeed, it is life and intellect and, we might add, will. For since it clearly directs all things to their respective ends, it has undoubtedly foreseen the end and willed it: indeed, it always foresees it and wills it, just as order is always maintained intact within all individual beings, and even when it seems to be interrupted it is re-instated more quickly than words can describe.

But we have no doubt at all that this is divine providence, providence which does not neglect even the tiniest things, for they have as much order as do the greatest, and which does not cease its work within the greatest things, for these, being very close to the controller, do not resist his control and are carefully arranged by that assent of the will through which they come into being and by which they are kept far from all harm.

Hence the statement: 'He dwells on high and regards the lowly in heaven and earth', just as heaven, while effortlessly pursuing its course within itself, at the same time floods the earth with the most abundant outpouring of its rays.

But at this point he says that law and skill depend on nature, or on nothing less than nature, because they are the offspring of the mind; you should understand that they are no less true than the forms of nature and that they take their birth from the divine intellect as their father and from the human mind as their mother. And you should mark our Plato's customary piety in calling upon God to give validity to the existence of the gods, I mean the one God, with the aim of teaching that all the gods are to be related to the one. Now he says that, trusting in the help of almighty God, he will discuss divine matters in complete safety.

To begin with, he condemns those natural philosophers who hold that the highest principles of creation are physical and that it is from these that life and intelligence came forth, when they should have said that physical things depend on intellectual life. That this is so he vows to demonstrate, not by a new opinion but by reason. For such a view was held by the ancient theologians prior to Plato, while the line of reasoning, such as will now begin from motion, is peculiar to Plato.

He divides motion into ten types: circuitous, transverse, thickening, thinning, increasing, decreasing, generative, decaying, changing from one thing to another, and changing from itself into itself and something different.

He marvels at circular motion, for it has an unmoving, indivisible centre, around which everything else moves. Again, in a sphere of vast extent innumerable circles can be traced, some greater than others.

And what is wonderful is that the smallest circle and the greatest circle complete their orbits simultaneously, so that within an integrated body the slow movement of one and the fast movement of the other are both to be wondered at, while the circles of medium size are related to medium speeds of movements in accordance with fixed proportions. We have dealt at length with this subject in our expositions in the *Theology*.

Now concerning that which changes its position, he says that it changes its centre, that is, the centre of its position, to which the circumference of the moving body is related; but sometimes, in addition to changing its centre, it somehow maintains the same centre, as when, not being fixed in place but transferred, it revolves through a comparable circumference.

Moreover, when he is speaking of creation, he says that as the principle, that is, the motivating and seminal nature, advances by means of change, it moves through the three dimensions of length, breadth, and depth; reaches quantity, quality, and a substantial form manifest to the senses through its effects; and attains being which has form, life, and perception.

Now his view is that in these movements the bodily mass is moved but does not impart movement; that bodily forms move masses and are moved by the soul; and that the soul moves both of these, although it itself is not moved by another but by itself; yet it imparts movement in such a way that as other things change so it itself is changed in its own way. He therefore considers the divine and angelic minds, which move what is lower but themselves remain completely unchanged, to be superior to souls. Finally, he deems the Good itself to be superior to these minds, for it is on account of the Good that all seek the truth.

Here he touches upon many things pertaining to self-moving nature, such as the true principle of movement and creation, in which some movement of form and some vital creation flourish of their own nature as models of all movement and creation. He declares that above all those things which are moved by outside agency there is a nature which is self-moving; and thus there is no need to embark on an infinite series.

On the contrary, beyond those things which shine or give warmth on account of something other than themselves, the journey can be made to that which shines by itself and gives heat by itself, and thus, beyond things that are moved by something else, that which is self-moving can be reached.

In fact, if all things were now at rest, and if something had soon to move before everything else, what would move first? It would not be the divine substance, which is totally motionless. And it would not be any physical things, which are moved by an outside agency. Therefore, only that which is self-moving would be the first to move, and by practising its movement within itself it would transfer it to other things, for it enables bodies to move, just as the unmoving principle of all things enables things to move.

But the soul's self-moving nature appears inwardly when it freely discourses and reasons and deliberates through its own nature; and it appears outwardly when, by its presence, it enables the body to move in some way of itself. However, we have dealt at great length in the *Theology* with all these matters and also with the fact that above the souls which rule the spheres there must needs be the angels and God.

But when Plato describes the soul as movement and creation, understand him to be indicating a cause, that is, the principle of movement and creation. And when he says that it moves by itself, he is referring to the reasoning power of the soul. Note at this point that it is said to be the reasoning power of the soul because it is able to move itself, lest you might think of the soul as the act of moving rather than as the non-contingent power to move. For in the same place he calls the soul substance.

You will thus come to this definition: The soul is a substance with its own power, by which it is moved of itself and by which it moves everything else.

But just as something which is self-moving precedes something which is moved by something else, so he thinks that the soul, I mean the rational soul, precedes the whole of the physical organism, since no body has the power to move of itself. The followers of Plato say that it precedes in importance as well as in time.

But if anyone wishes Plato to have less disagreement with the Christians, he should explain that our soul has precedence, either at a particular moment of time or at least in importance and according to the will of the Creator. Since the substance of the soul is prior to the substance of the body, he concludes that the states and movements and personal endowments of the soul are prior to the affections of the body.

When he mentions the property of the soul, remember that those things which indicate action are common both to our soul and to the

141

gods above, while those things which indicate passion are common to both our soul and to the lowest daemons. Natural movement, however, which is an effect in the body, is an action within the soul; and that which is length, breadth, depth, quality, and movement within the body is, within the soul, incisiveness, judgement, memory, character, and disposition. In the *Theology* you have a clearer exposition of other matters of this kind.

He says that the soul is also the cause of evils, I mean through accident, and that our soul has free will. Be on your guard when he says that the world is governed by the soul, that is, by its own soul, because he adds that the soul is double: one soul is beneficent, while the other is the opposite, lest you should understand a double substance rather than a double power, for in the soul of the world and in the celestial soul there is power. One is the mover of bodies, while the other is intellectual.

The intellectual one is undoubtedly beneficent, arranging all things in good order, while the mover is beneficent, that is, it puts things into good order, insofar as it is subordinate to the first. But if it were not subordinate to the first, then the more effective it is in imparting movement, the more strongly, through lack of skill, would it hurl the universe into confusion.

But that the celestial soul has a mind he demonstrates from the order which he never fails to observe in every movement and act of creation. Indeed, the insane are, as we can see, the more estranged from the mind the more they are estranged from order.

For the moment, we describe order as the connecting link between things and actions, a link positioned according to a harmonious series, directed by its own reason towards a definite end and preserving in all things, as far as is possible, that which is similar, equal, and identical. We see that order of this kind is kept only by those who are sound in mind, and that it is directly fulfilled in the actual development of the universe: fulfilled, I say, with the highest level of efficiency and beauty. From all this it is apparent that it is governed from a soul which possesses a mind of supreme accomplishment and excellence.

Nor does he miss the target when he says that the circle is proper to the mind, for in the circle the indivisible centre remains still, while the circumference moves around it, and in this shape and movement equality is maintained.

In the mind, likewise, watchfulness directed towards the truth remains simple and steadfast, while the causes unfold, through intermediaries, into effects, and the effects, in their turn, are likewise taken back into their causes. Meanwhile, the attention of the mind returns to a consideration of itself and moves forward in a measured progression, with a similar, equal, and identical aim, by perceiving, willing, and acting.

But after he has shown that the celestial spheres are endowed with souls, and that souls are endowed with excellent minds, and after he has demonstrated that the universe is moved by a single soul, and that the numerous spheres are moved by many souls, he now briefly distinguishes the three ways in which souls may be united with celestial beings.

He says that the soul may be within the sphere, just as our soul is within the body, so that a single living being is produced thereby; or that the soul is present in such a way that it does not actually enliven the sphere but merely moves it and rules it, either through some wonderful motive power or through some other medium.

Although Plato does not at this point clearly select one of these three proposals in preference to the others, all his followers unhesitatingly choose the first, and they consider Aristotle and Theophrastus to have held exactly the same view; for they think that Plato quite likely held this view, because the line of reasoning by which he endows heaven with a soul suggests that the soul itself is moved when heaven is moved, since if a single living being were not produced from the soul and the sphere there would certainly not be a moving mover, but a motionless mover.

This is what he re-asserts in the *Phaedrus* and also in the *Timaeus*, where he says: 'Since the maker of the world wanted to make the world an intelligent living being, and since the intellect could not be present in the body without some intermediary, he joined the intellect to the soul, and the soul to the body, and he did this so thoroughly that he poured it into the centre of the world and from there he diffused it throughout all the parts.'

But in any case, why does Plato at this point openly confirm only the celestial gods? It is because contemplation of the gods is far removed from the substance of the laws, and through the celestial gods, which are moved and which are committed to their respective functions, he gives sufficient indication that there is something higher to be sought which, remaining motionless itself, moves all the others and, as the leader of all, assigns to all others their respective duties.

What further? He has clearly shown that above the celestial souls dwell the divine mind and the angelic minds, for he says that the celestial soul, which, of course, does not exist of itself if it accepts the perennially divine intellect, guides all things aright, insofar as what is right and happy is considered to reside with the gods; and if not, it goes gravely astray. For this reason, when Plato moves from the soul to the mind, like someone moving up from the eye to a higher light, he is very much afraid that he will be dazzled.

But after he has shown that the gods exist, he proves that they provide, taking as his starting-point this remarkable statement: A nature which is akin to divinity leads men who have not fallen short of the human race in all respects to affirm that God exists, although the apparent prosperity of the wicked – a false prosperity which in due time will bring punishment – may make us entertain doubts about the providence of God.

If God creates by understanding, it follows that He understands what He creates; and if He creates everything, then He understands everything. If He knows the whole, He also knows the parts of which the whole necessarily consists. If He knows the parts, then He knows the details of which the parts necessarily consist. One, therefore, who has the power and the knowledge to provide also has the power and the knowledge to rule the universe.

It is also His will to govern the whole of His work advantageously. But He can never govern it well unless the parts are governed. In the same way, neither the physician nor the architect can take the best care of the whole without caring for the parts which necessarily contribute to the whole. God does not fail to govern the smallest things, for He did not fail to create them. Government is not difficult for God to exercise, just as creation is not difficult for Him.

Gentleness does not make Him slow to exercise care, for He is the strongest of all and He governs all things with greater care than art or nature show towards their creations. For to the extent that the works of God depend upon God more than the works of art or nature depend upon art or nature, to the same extent does God provide more carefully for His works, and it is through His providence that all things are able to provide in the same way for whatever is in their care.

But since the ease with which art accomplishes things both great and small increases with the growing maturity of the art, the art within God, being limitless, undoubtedly governs the smallest things and the greatest things with the utmost ease, and in organising them it assuredly organises the parts for the benefit of the whole, rather than the whole for the benefit of the parts, and it relates the good of each part to the good of the whole.

But of all the things under the Moon, the greatest care is taken of the human race, because it is the most complete and because it worships God, as if it were especially honoured by God. You will note here that for every kind and species within the creation God has arranged rulers or guardians, even for the smallest actions and effects. For just as it is through His power that they are enabled to do whatever they can, so it is through His providence, which cares for even the smallest things, that they are also able to care for the smallest things.

You will note that, as Plotinus and Hermias also maintain, the senses – particularly sight and hearing – are in the stars, but they are in a category that far exceeds the senses of earthly creatures.

You will also note that the human soul is always united to a body and constantly united to an ethereal body, but alternately to an earthy body and an airy body.

Again, you will observe that the movement of the soul – being first, spontaneous, and therefore free – can be led into different forms, in such a way that at one time it is changed into a condition lower than the human, and at another time into a condition higher than the human, going down from the one to lower positions as if by some weightiness, and rising up from the other, as if by some lightness, to seek what is above.

From this it is clear that conditions produced from specific movements are in accordance with divine will through law; for just as that law ordains that things celestial are suited to good souls, while things terrestrial are suited to evil souls, so, with absolutely no external impulse, but as if following a natural instinct, the conditions of the good spontaneously seek what is above, while those of the bad fall to what is below.

If it were proper at this point to comment at greater length, I should certainly expound that very abstruse statement which he makes when he presents someone who is attempting to transmute fire into living water as one who is toiling at a most arduous task; for since water is opposed to fire, and life cannot be created out of fire, a man who is striving to transmute fire into living water is undoubtedly attempting the impossible.

And there is another statement, no less obscure, which should be expounded in relation to dialectical synthesis and division. Of course, if one follows a three-stage process of division, moving from a very common genus to subordinate species, and from them to sub-species, this is an easy process of division. Likewise, if one re-traces the same steps, moving from the sub-species to the sub-genus, and thence to the common genus, this, too, is a simple process of synthesis. However, anyone who wishes to move through all individual things, which are limitless in number, will be attempting a vain undertaking. But more on these matters in the commentaries to the *Philebus*.

Among other things, you will observe some words of Plato that are very similar to the utterance of the prophet David: Neither by ascending to heaven nor by descending to hell can divine judgement be avoided.

He then shows that God cannot be unjustly placated by gifts from corrupt men. When you consider that God cares for the human race more lovingly than shepherds care for their sheep, helmsmen for their ships, generals for their armies, countrymen for their fields, charioteers for their horses, and doctors for their patients; that all things under heaven are full of evils; and that around souls rages everlasting warfare, in which vices drag downwards, while gods and daemons lift upwards, you will observe that within God are the living virtues, indeed, lives themselves, by some of whose sparks, kindled within the soul, the soul is raised aloft.

But after these preambles he turns his attention, with a somewhat strict appraisal, to the irreligious, and he carefully examines not only wicked actions but also verbal effrontery and even thoughts against the sublime nature of God; and he changes the three types of irreligion, mentioned earlier, into six, by dividing each one into two. For those three comprise a false view opposed to God; but as an accompaniment to a false view there can also be an imbalance in life and character; there can be a more acceptable balance, too.

You will also find here the punishments for evil-doers, for superstitious heretics, and for those who are known as false prophets. He also condemns popular superstition, and he has already condemned poetic superstition, by which popular superstition is reinforced. But Plato always condemns superstition, both poetic and popular, and he honours philosophical piety as the highest of all human duties.

The Theme of the
Eleventh Book of the *Laws*

OUR PLATO, the wisest of all philosophers, the most eloquent of orators, and the most prudent of all lawyers – wishing to avoid being needlessly compelled, like all others, to concoct a vast work of laws and their interpretations in relation to contracts – quite rightly made it his endeavour, before limiting himself to contracts and legal and commercial matters, to create good citizens by means of disciplines, laws, legal proceedings, and religion, in the hope that just men, even without the need for laws, would of their own initiative prove their loyalty and truthfulness in all business dealings.

And indeed, after the laws concerning proceedings which relate to persons, he very properly focuses on laws of judgements relating to things, by which both strangers and citizens may learn the just way to make and safeguard deposits and compacts; not to disturb other people's property, but to render to each his own in the case of children, freedmen, and slaves; to sell, buy, and restore; to lead and to serve as a soldier; to protect minors; to make a will and keep it; to administer inheritances; to make a marriage contract and a settlement of divorce; to govern a family; but, above all, to honour one's parents conscientiously; to corrupt nothing; to abhor sorcery, avoid anger and folly, and shun disputes, affronts, and disparagements; to repay losses; and to keep the truth in giving evidence and in taking oaths. This is really the whole subject matter of the eleventh book.

But at this point we think that we should briefly expound, as we usually do, some of the aspects which are not so clear.

Firstly, you should know that the goddess of travel has two functions: to show and to preserve. The first, under the name of the Moon, is light, and the second, under the name of Diana, is trust; and anything strange that is encountered by chance on a journey should be devoted to God, so that you may acknowledge that good fortune is to be ascribed to the providence of God.

Consider the goodness of Plato's teaching, which, in buying and selling, prohibits us not only from debasing a commodity, making false promises, and swearing falsely, but even from swearing at all; indeed, it prohibits us from praising the object being sold and from exchanging it for money on the same day. For this is what he teaches when he says,

'No one must tell a lie to the gods who have been invoked, or practise deception, or debase in words; or dare to do anything unless he wishes to be hated by God, who hates firstly the man who despises the gods by swearing falsely, and secondly the man who gives a false picture of himself before the elders.'

. And see, again and again, what free and wholesome minds Plato selects from among the citizens, by means of which he drives far away all opportunity for petty dealings.

He adds that both sumptuousness and destitution constitute mental sickness; for from the former men become overblown, and from the latter they become weak and wretched.

But when he says that Pallas, Vulcan, and Mars preside over the arts, you should gather, from the numerous secret sayings of Plato which have been transmitted in one place or another, that a trinity of divine beings, which in Platonic terminology we call the workforce, always assists Jupiter, the supreme maker of the universe. In this trinity Pallas is first, Vulcan is second, and Mars is third. But just as the whole trinity is related to Jupiter, from whom it arises, so Vulcan and Mars are fully related to Pallas.

At this point I briefly touch upon the fact that power seems to have slumbered and dreamt within Mars, wisdom within Pallas, and a fiery spirit within Vulcan.

Three things are certainly required for the skilful work of Jupiter, by which everything is perfected. The first is reason herself, by means of which he is going to make every single thing. The second is the effective preparation of those things which he has conceived through reason. The third is the welfare and protection of those things which are ready to be despatched into manifestation.

The Idea of the first he calls Pallas; of the second, Vulcan; of the third, Mars. And because each one – preservation, defence, and despatch (or the expression of creation) — is in need of reason and wisdom, Pallas is before Vulcan and Mars, and whatever is forged by Vulcan or by Mars, once it has been made, is protected and preserved in its proper form, being brought to fulfilment by Pallas, the leader.

But these three who preside over divine art leave three traces in nature, as we can see: Pallas leaves order, by which all things are arranged; Vulcan leaves effective development and a ready birth, to which all things hasten; and Mars leaves a well-fortified structure provided by parents for their offspring, as well as various bulwarks to defend one's own nature against opposing forces.

These three must likewise be in all human art, but especially in the art of civil government, so that every single thing is wisely thought out before being made; every single thing is prepared expeditiously and vigorously; every single thing is expressed in that form in which it was conceived; and it is then preserved and stoutly protected.

And in order that we may understand that, in bringing all things to perfection, human art depends no less than nature does on God Himself and on Ideas, he says that those three divinities preside over human arts. But to prevent us from thinking that only the arts come from the gods, he adds that the gods should be so greatly honoured above all as the bestowers of life that their names are not to be uttered brazenly or rashly, but all matters pertaining to them are to be handled with purity, reverence, and integrity.

Nothing can be conceived that is more virtuous than these precepts, if only he had related them to God rather than to the gods. But, in fact, he has established the single substance of supreme Jupiter, and he has not introduced many substances while introducing many Ideas. What more do we expect from him? In fact, when he refers to gods, his thoughts are those of the man who said, 'Thousand thousands ministered unto him.'

Nor should we forbear to mention that when it is said that the soul receives life from God, life is to be understood as the mean between that life which abides in eternity, such as angelic life in its fullness, and that life which is enclosed within specific parameters of time. It is the mean, I repeat, because it is composed of eternity and time. Its substance, like that of heaven, always abides, while its actions and characteristics are in continual flux. And this is why, in the previous book, he said that the soul both is and comes into being at the same time; that it is imperishable but not eternal (which is the law by which the gods exist), that is, not permanent in all respects.

Yet he has said that the gods, that is, the angels, abide, meaning that they abide not of themselves but by virtue of the divine law, which of itself keeps them moving throughout eternity.

When he says that their body, too, is imperishable, he means, of course, their celestial body. But perhaps he also means their elemental body, insofar as the mass of the elements and primordial matter are not destroyed. In the *Statesman* he says that it is from these that the same body is divinely re-created at some time.

You will mark that when he speaks of wills, the person and property of any citizen do not belong to the citizen but to the country. Again, when the care of orphans is being dealt with, he says that the souls of the dead are alive to our affairs and take care of them, that is, they are in touch with them through their celestial and airy body, and they take care of some things before others, being more strongly drawn towards them by nature, familiarity, or divine providence.

This is especially true of those souls which, although they have held on to life, also attain the middle region: middle both in position and in character, for the position is between heaven and earth, and the character is between highest bliss and extreme wretchedness. For it is important to remember what was said in the previous book: that just as souls, having been made from themselves to be such as they are, then move, through the principle of similarity, to the levels and positions and so on of those that are similar to themselves, in the same way those that have been made celestial seek the celestial, while the earthy seek the earthy, and the airy seek the airy.

Indeed, although Plato does not venture to make other statements about souls, yet to this extent, both here and in the book *On Knowledge*, he makes his statements very clearly and often indicates as much elsewhere.

Hence he also says that we should beware of harming our pupils, lest the souls of their parents be justly angry with us. And we find the same in the ninth book, where, in dealing with homicides, he says that the souls are aggrieved by their killers. Similar to this is the statement, 'The souls of Marius' men troubled Sulla, and tragedies pursued the frenzied Orestes hence.'

Then you will observe that when he is dealing with the honour due to parents, the statues of the gods are to be honoured, not in themselves but because they show us the gods; yet parents are to receive greater honour, as if they were the living images of the gods. He adds that the curses of the parents upon their children are heard by God and that nothing more disastrous can befall children.

After much intervening material you will hear once more something that is strongly characteristic of Plato. Unkind people are troubled with punishments, not because they have done something (for what is done cannot be undone), but to prevent something similar from being done in the future and to ensure that those who are punished should pursue injustice with hatred, or at least should not fall again into a similar fault.

He also says that the judge is the interpreter of the lawgiver and the servant of justice. He then administers punishment to tale-bearers, disparagers, those who strike in anger, those who utter abuse, those who offend venerable people with caustic jests, and those who become bitterly angry in playful situations. You will hear that what should inspire the greatest fear is divine retribution when perjury has been committed in the giving of evidence or in the swearing of oaths.

Finally, you will hear that in giving evidence and taking oaths the truth itself is always to be established through Themis, Jupiter, and Apollo: through Themis, who represents law and right, both secular and sacred, so that anyone who lies while taking an oath or giving evidence before men or God may understand that he is committing a grave offence against human law and right in the sight of men, and against divine law and right in the sight of God; through Jupiter, who makes everything tremble with a nod of his head, so that anyone who has sinned may realise that he will by no means avoid the retribution wrought by divine power; and through Phoebus, lest the offender should trust that his offences, present or past, can lie hidden from him who, through prophecy, foretells all that is to come.

The Theme of the
Twelfth Book of the *Laws*

IN ALL HIS BOOKS of the *Laws*, the divine Plato, imitating the work of God, and therefore finding delight in the number twelve, wished the twelfth book to be the common repository for all the laws, just as the twelfth sphere of the world is the common firmament for all the stars.

And just as anyone who penetrates the twelfth sphere will at once find fulfilment and happiness for his soul and embrace them, so Plato, wishing to move beyond the twelfth book, will show in the *Epinomis* not so much the laws themselves as the blessed fulfilment of the soul that has been attained through the laws.

In the earlier books, the laws deal partly with public duties and partly with private transactions, partly with home affairs and partly with foreign affairs, both in times of peace and in times of war. But in the twelfth book they are all gathered together somehow, being relevant to all situations. I do not mean all the individual laws, but some from each category.

To the laws is added the most important factor of all: reason, the preserver and reformer of the laws. To the magistrates, too, is added the most important factor: the principle of accounting for their actions and having them examined, which is considered the highest public duty performed by the magistrates, just as the examination of one's conscience is considered the highest personal action performed by souls.

The entire health of souls certainly consists in this personal examination, and the entire health of the State consists in this public examination. And this is the subject matter, in brief, of the twelfth book.

But since, quite near the beginning as well as in later dialogues and earlier ones, he mentions the children of the gods and calls some gods the children of others, while he calls men the children of the gods, it should be remembered that, in Plato's writings, there are two ways in which the gods are the children of other gods, and there are also two ways in which men are the children of the gods.

First of all, as the *Timaeus* teaches, all the rulers of the spheres of the world – both the actual rulers of the spheres of the world and the actual souls of the spheres, both the daemons on this side of the spheres and the angelic intellects beyond the spheres – are the children of almighty God, being begotten by His gracious will.

Secondly, in any one of these three categories, those that are lower are called the children of those that are higher, because as they unceasingly receive rays and forms from those above them they are thereby somehow given form and seem to comply with them as if with their fathers.

Men, likewise, are said to have been begotten by the gods, either because they have been brought into the light from the beginning of creation out of the bowels of the earth to be a solace for the gods or because some of them, being daily moved by the inspiration of the gods, are quickly and divinely transposed, as if re-born, from their normal human condition to some divine state of life, at which level Plato frequently places both dutiful philosophers and philosophical rulers.

Now because, at the beginning of the book, he puts Jupiter and Mercury in authority over ambassadors and heralds, Jupiter is to be understood firstly as God, the Maker of the world, and Mercury is to be understood as the whole order of angels; and Jupiter is to be understood secondly as the favourable planet indicating rulers and laws, while Mercury is to be understood as a different planet indicating the fulfilment of interpretation and efficiency.

I describe the planets as indicators because, as Timaeus witnesses and as Plotinus reasons, the planets and all celestial phenomena indicate and announce, as far as they can, either what the gods will shortly do or what we ourselves in the meantime intend to do or rather, as often happens, what we are going to suffer.

It is not long before he expresses his condemnation of the poets who, imputing to the gods the wrong-doings of men, fail to show respect for the divine nature and at the same time seriously corrupt human beings with the bad example of the gods.

Moreover, he thinks that thefts and other offences merit more censure in relation to the sinner's intention and practice, healthy or unhealthy, than in relation to his character.

Among the laws pertaining to military service he ordains what is thought to be the best thing of all in every life, namely, that no one should know his own span of life or do anything in isolation from others, but that all and sundry should direct their actions in accordance with the will of someone wise or superior and for the general welfare.

He teaches that the judges should not overstep the law in passing sentence, either of their own volition or under compulsion. For in the view of the ancients, particularly that of Orpheus and Hesiod, judgement itself is a pure maiden. In the face of purity and judgement a lie is the most hateful thing of all. They consider that the goddess who presides over judgement is divine Providence, to be held in reverence by human judges.

Later, when he condemns those who have disgraced themselves by flinging their weapons to the ground, and also those generals who enlist those soldiers once more to serve under their banners, they receive what we have translated here as a fine of ten minae, but which is stated elsewhere by the laws to be one thousand minae.

A little later he affirms that the court of appeal is well known to the State, so that no one in the State may be a judge unless there be another judge. If this is not the case, then, through unrestrained freedom in making judgements, justice will perish and the State, lacking justice as its soul, will die.

But he understands the temple of the Sun and of Apollo to be dedicated not only to the solar planet and its soul but much more to the light of the Highest Good, whose image is the Sun.

You will hear that errors are committed in judgements when religion is not present; but that the worst of all irreligious men are those who trust so strongly in their ability to appease God with their entreaties and sacrifices that on account of such trust they believe they have the right to extort large sums of money with impunity.

After this he imparts the very prudent laws that concern the acceptance of foreigners and the travels made by citizens to other countries, lest the customs of the citizens be disturbed by some foreign and ill-advised practice, or the expertise of foreigners be unavailable to the State. You will note at this point that within some corrupt people, too, a divine force is present, by means of which they can discern the possibilities of human talents, for he shows that something of the divine nature is not only acquired by us but is also, if I may express it like this, born within us.

He directs that it is not to be treated as a trifling matter whether you appear upright or not, but a reputation for virtue should be sought, and it should be sought through virtue alone.

He sometimes records that divine men appear among the common people or within States that are badly governed.

After this he deals with many points concerning court cases, accusation, defence, appeal, surety, proscription, and other such matters.

He takes this opportunity to state, in the midst of these words, which parts of the temple and which images should be dedicated to the gods, and to say what the symbolic teaching is, according to the Pythagorean ceremonies.

He says that the Earth and Vesta form the sacred dwelling-place for all the gods. By adding Vesta he indicated that the name 'Earth' should be understood at a deeper level to include this elemental earth, the lunar earth, and finally the starry earth. There are also three souls and three angels for the three earths.

But remember that, according to the ancients, anything in the universe that is effective in shaping and moving is described metaphorically as fire; again, anything anywhere that is very easily fashioned is said to be air; anything purifying is said to be water; and anything solid or stable and fixed is called earth.

A nature which has a dense or fixed quality, whether it be here, in the Moon, or in the vault of heaven, is called earth by the followers of

Plato. Who will then be surprised to hear that the Earth is the sacred dwelling-place for all the gods, if the universe is contained within the three boundaries of the three earths?

And since he has said that it was consecrated to the gods from the beginning, he forbids it to be re-consecrated, with the warning that you are not to entrust anything to God which is not already God's. He also forbids the making of statues from gold or silver, to prevent us from feeling confident that through their great value we shall redeem ourselves from great sins. He further forbids the making of statues from ivory, since ivory has been deprived of sensory life, and thus he prevents us from engaging in religion without sense, that is, without vigilance and awareness. He also rejects bronze and iron, condemning them as instruments of war. For we offer sacrifices in vain if our heart makes division between ourselves and others. In short, he is willing to accept wood and stone as materials for making images of the gods: in stone he commends the steadfastness of the mind in holy rituals, and in wood he commends the food of fire, that is, the blazing heat of the soul, which is easily kindled in holy ceremonies. His direction is that complete images should be fashioned either from stone or from wood, and above all he commends simplicity and purity.

And we should not pass over in silence the fact that envoys had been sent earlier to four oracles, that we might acknowledge that God, the Maker of all, provides equally for all parts of the world, which are portrayed as the four corners known as East, West, North, and South, and that any ceremony with which God is worshipped with a pure mind and for His own sake is to some extent acceptable to God. But we have written more fully about these matters elsewhere.

Meanwhile, he forbids those who serve their country in any matter to accept gifts. He also deals with taxes. He says that no one can learn anything better than that which will make them better. He says that the law is something to marvel at, that it is divine, and that among the Greeks it takes its name from the mind itself: from the divine mind, its father, and from the human mind, its mother. Now he would like judgement to follow the law, for these two are the greatest benefits for mankind.

But at this point he returns to the mind, because at the end of the eleventh book he says that our possessions are spoilt mostly by some inherent diseases. And he says elsewhere that the disease of the law is the dishonesty of its own magistrates, while the disease of judgement and judicial arbitration he has in the same place called the expertise of the barrister, which, through no established principle of law but through the eagerness prompted by greed and ambition, agrees to defend indiscriminately any cause which is despised above all others as a plague on the State.

Later, when he is prescribing laws for funeral ceremonies, he particularly wishes the man himself to be considered as the substance of the rational soul, and the body to be considered as an image of this man, or, as he calls it elsewhere, the shadow of the man. From the *Timaeus, Alcibiades*, and Plotinus we learn about what is human within us and what is creaturely, and we have spoken more fully of this in the *Theology*, where he concludes that man is indeed the substance of the rational soul, beyond reason, and having, in addition, some sense that is very deep within, impassible, and neutral, while what is creaturely is composed of the body that has been formed and the trace of life that has been imprinted by the soul.

Within this trace the second sense has been impressed by the first sense and distributed in a passible state through various instruments. This seems to be in harmony with some of the sayings made by St Paul; but when he says that the soul departs to other gods when about to give an account of its deeds, he calls the other gods angelic minds beyond physical bodies: there are said to be other gods, which are beyond the souls of the spheres. Since our souls, conjoined to these bodies, are undoubtedly positioned below the realm of the higher souls, they are, when detached, transferred to the jurisdiction of those who are detached.

Up to this point he has established laws, but he says that laws are made in vain unless consideration is given to the security and steadfastness of the laws. He will therefore set up an extraordinary assembly of magistrates to ensure their stability. But before creating such an assembly, he touches a little on the power of the fates, as you might expect from someone who understands that the wisdom of men is not sufficient to ensure the human security of such a great task if the power of the fates is decidedly unfavourable.

With these words he certainly seems to approve of those who, in founding cities, establishing laws, electing magistrates, and even cultivating men, carefully avoid the highly adverse dispositions of the stars. On the subject of fate, much is said elsewhere, in conformity with which the following statements are put forward with as much pertinence as brevity. Fate is an unchanging disposition in the soul of the world of change. The instrument of fate is celestial nature. But the matter upon which it acts as an instrument is the mass of the elements.

He accepts the three names of Lachesis, Clotho, and Atropos as pertaining both to the instrument and to matter. For we may call Lachesis the firmament, within whose stars the powers and destinies of all the lower beings are held. We may regard Clotho as the assembly of planets assisting the firmament in unfolding the destinies of things. And, finally, we may see Atropos as Saturn in particular, inexorably corroborating with its own steadiness the destinies which have been brought into manifestation.

Within the substance of fate, too, we include the three Fates, since the force of fate, permeating the elements through the celestial instrument, influences matter and form and compounds, as well as essence, power, and action, and the beginning, the middle, and the end. But since it acts not only upon bodies but also upon minds, inasmuch as minds are affected by bodies or make use of them, Plato says here that the Fates have the power to safeguard the welfare of bodies, souls, and laws.

And since the mind, through its own nature, trusts in the providence of the divine mind from time to time, as you might expect, and thus either overpowers fate or turns fate to good account, he added that, for the welfare of life both public and private, sense should be conjoined with mind in such a way that it submits to the mind and ministers to it.

Similar to this link between mind and sight and hearing is the assembly of magistrates which he creates to ensure the stability of the laws within the State: an assembly which will first consider the aim of the State, and then the best ways of achieving this aim; which will strive in all respects to ensure that whatever is done within the State, both privately and publicly, will, through a single principle, lead to the One; and which will direct all things towards virtue, all the virtues towards prudence, and prudence towards wisdom, which is signified here by the word 'mind'. By this single principle, all the virtues are considered to receive full acclaim, inasmuch as they lead to wisdom, which receives his approval because it partakes of the one divine Good.

He declares that it is a most refined view of creation which sees the many as many but at the same time sees that there is one common nature within all things; that they have received this nature from a single source; and that through this nature they are able to lead to a single end.

Without a reflection of this kind no one is able to govern his life perfectly, either in private or in public Since this reflection is particularly the province of the divine philosopher, it is not without justification that he deems that, of all the citizens gathered together in that most select assembly, the divine philosophers are the ones to whom the highest of matters should be referred: I mean the divine observers and devotees of things divine.

And this is why he wards off from the most wide-ranging functions of the State all those who are slow to contemplate the divine, sluggish in worshipping the divine, or ill-equipped to teach the divine.

But he soon goes on to show that two things in particular are essential to undeviating faith in the supreme divinity. Firstly, we should know that the level of rational souls is divine and of greater antiquity than physical bodies: by it are the spheres moved, and by it is everything within the spheres begotten. Secondly, we should consider that the level of angelic minds is above the level of souls. It is only through partaking of mind that souls can move the spheres in their due order. Anyone who knows these two things will easily understand that just as the mind is the form and order of the soul, so the divine Good is the life and light of both mind and soul.

There is no doubt that in almost all of his writings Plato either demonstrates or intimates that these three – the divine Good, the mind, and the soul – are the principles of all things. This is what he wraps up in somewhat opaque verbiage in his letter to Dionysius.

But if it is not appropriate to say that our soul is older in time than our body, let us at least say that it is of greater importance and therefore first, because it takes its rise from a principle higher than that of physical bodies, and this is why movement in the soul comes from itself, while movement in the body comes from the soul. And because changeability increases within the body, he says that the body depends not only on the changeable action of the soul but also on changeable substance.

And he reproves Anaxagoras because, not having positioned the soul between mind and body, he was obliged to state that natural dispositions are not arranged by intelligence through the soul (although they are), but occur through elemental nature.

But Plato states here, as he does in the *Timaeus* and in the *Phaedo*, that all things are appointed to happen either through angelic minds, through souls, or through bodies, and especially through divine will and the grace of the Good.

PART THREE

The Commentary of Marsilio Ficino
to Plato's *Epinomis*

A Summary of *Epinomis,*
a philosophical appendix to the *Laws*

NO FOLLOWER of Plato doubts, great-souled Lorenzo, that the treasury of the divine Plato lies buried in this work called *Epinomis*, which is also entitled *The Philosopher*. But to unearth it fully, many devices are needed.

Yet it is not right for your Marsilio, who is setting forth the contents, to present them at great length, especially since the couriers from the scribes and printers are persistently pressing for the work: wresting the summaries importunately from our hands, they scarcely allow us to pursue the main points in the individual volumes.

The direction given by the preceding *Laws* is to strive to the utmost to compose the minds of the citizens, so that, having attained an easy tranquillity, they may carefully investigate the principles and causes of divine works and in them, as if in mirrors, descry and worship God the Creator.

Indeed, within reflection there is wisdom, within worship there is religion, and within both lie the whole of human happiness and the end of the laws. The higher laws, in fact, promise this kind of fulfilment, while *Epinomis* fulfils the promise through the gift of God. And so, having prophesied this perfect condition of the mind at the beginning of the work, Plato then devoutly begs for it from God.

Some have judged that happiness can be enjoyed in this life; others, in another life; and yet others, never. Of course, any who think that it can be acquired in this life through human exertion, while the evidence of their whole life cries out in protest, are clearly mistaken. But those who think that it can never be acquired are empty and would make the impulse of the whole of nature empty, too.

Very wisely does our Plato hope that happiness can be attained in the next life, both through the virtues of the present life and through the gift of God. However, he is not without faith that some rare souls, such as he speaks of in the *Phaedrus*, the *Phaedo*, and the *Republic*, can enjoy happiness in this very life, living outside the body rather than within the body, and living for God rather than for themselves, with the result that, through the gracious favour of God, they seem to sip the ethereal nectar even in the midst of the very waves of Lethe.

It is not without justification that he has added the word 'Philosopher' to the title of *Epinomis*, since, as is clear in the sixth and seventh books of the *Republic*, as well as in the present work, the function of the philosopher is to enquire into the principles of all things, in order to find the divine principle by which they are made; to worship this principle once it has been found; and to enjoy it after worshipping it.

However, in this book, while he strives to guide us to happiness, which he unhesitatingly locates within religious wisdom, he depicts the mind of the true student of philosophy, and he instructs and shapes it through appropriate stages of training. And in all situations, not less but much more virtue and piety than knowledge are expected of the philosopher. And whatever be the knowledge that he expects from him, he requires him to worship God, before all others, as the true Teacher of knowledge and as the Maker of all that is known.

But first he shows that the power to attain divine bliss has been naturally implanted within us, for in all our actions we all proclaim and seek this power, and we are fulfilled by nought else. Secondly, while enumerating our capabilities one by one in due order, he shows that this power is not acquired through our natural or vital faculties, or through our light-hearted, playful, and subordinate faculties. Thirdly, he shows that wisdom and piety, the foundations of bliss, are attained through both the moral virtues and the contemplative virtues.

But when he enumerates the speculative branches of learning, he not only praises arithmetic first of all but actually marvels at it, for in his earlier writings he says that arithmetic, more than anything else, sharpens the mind, strengthens the memory, and makes the spirit most efficient and ready to accomplish any reflection and any action. And at this point he adds that number has been given to men by God Himself as the indispensable instrument of reason and discourse. If it were removed, the spirit would appear mindless and the sciences and arts would altogether vanish.

He goes on to praise geometry, which considers measures; stereometry, which gauges weights; astronomy, which observes the heavens; and music, which imitates the harmony of the heavens.

He also commends natural science when it deals with types of bodies, with compounds, living creatures, and the principles of motion and of generation, but in such a way that it leaves all the details of natural things for the physicians, as if they were far removed from a man who has recourse to the divine.

And, lastly, he puts above everything dialectic, that is, metaphysics, with theology at its apex like a queen, because it uses all individual things as steps leading to the discovery and worship of God.

Now he shows that there are three functions performed by this queen concerning her remaining powers. The first is that she looks upon the vast multitude of all these things. The second is that she perceives that within all these things there is but a single common factor and connection. The third is that she clearly observes the principle by which the multitude, and that which unites it, lead to the One Itself, the divine Good. But he adds that, unless there is an understanding of this principle which unites the branches of learning and leads to the divine One, the other sciences will turn out to be totally empty; and nothing in them can be perceived as the One unless they are established in relation to the One, from which they receive that very factor which unites them.

But the mind has obtained all this, and in being thus united to itself it is re-united through itself to God; and he says that it is as blissful as it can be in this life, and that it will be totally blissful in the next life. Now such is the theme of the whole book. Shortly after the beginning, where the words of our translation are 'Time is brief' (the words which follow can be read elsewhere), it seems to be abandoned in relation to the proper discourse of reason, not only in depraved men but also in temperate men.

But when he praises heaven as the cause of prudence and of all good things, this is the type of praise he intends to be transferred from the corporeal heaven to the incorporeal heaven, that is, to the Idea of heaven. In the same place he directs that this Idea be honoured by means of the visible heaven, as if it were made known by its image.

But take note at this point that men are considered to be within the race of terrestrial daemons, for he says 'All other daemons together' and so on. Then he says that anyone who knew that which is divine through the action of generation would know true number and holiness. The 'divine within generation' means two things: firstly, a kind of spirited movement which is within the soul, or some power which impels bodily movement and is the origin of generation; and secondly, the natural species which is preserved in the unending succession of generation.

Now within the movement of the soul there is true number, which harmonises, as the *Timaeus* says, through musical proportion and concord. Within species there is also true number; for the species of all things are disposed according to definite number and order. Religion is confirmed by both of these, for from the free movement of the soul we can infer the divine substance which is self-existent, and from the unbroken continuance of Ideas within species we can surmise eternity.

You will hear a similar view expressed in the sacred words of Moses, for he says that if any evil is inflicted upon us from the qualities of the air or from plants and animals, divine nature is not to blame: the responsibility lies with human nature, which organises its life without regard for justice.

In the words that follow, you will clearly recognise the aim of the laws. This aim has been expounded to you that you may, by worshipping God and by living a pure life, attain a death which is excellent and full of beauty.

Next, he repeats the three fundamental aspects of religion. The first is to believe in God. The second is to admit that both the greatest and the smallest things are in His care. The third is never to suppose that God is swayed by any prayers or gifts.

He reinforces faith in the divine nature by pointing to the wonderfully divine nature of the soul itself. But he thinks that for anything better than the body to be more divine, too – that is, more akin to the divine than to the corporeal – it must also be older than all bodies, because within every kind or order in the creation that which is closer to perfection also possesses a greater degree of being; and this is why he presents to imperfect beings the cause of existence. That which is the cause of something else is certainly anterior to it.

He adds that when a living creature is formed from the conjoining of the soul with the body, a single form then manifests in the body: a physical life, existing within a subject and proceeding from the advent of incorporeal life. He posits two kinds of things: one corporeal, and the other incorporeal. To the latter he adds action, and to the former he adds passivity. He says that the form of the incorporeal is single, the main reason being that it is simple and always endures within the very form of substance. But the words 'For it is not other', and so on, are to be found elsewhere as 'For that which is changed into something other is not the incorporeal, which is quite devoid of colour and which transcends the most divine level of the soul.'

164

Now at the level of body he locates five bodies, which he calls solids because, having the dimension of depth, they are clearly different from planes; and within every body, even the most fluid, there is something solid, on account of the consistency of its own nature and, in Platonic terms, on account of a similarity of earthly nature extending as far as the sky.

To the sky he gives the name of fire, because it has its own light, and light is a specific property of fire. The sky is also engaged in everlasting movement, such as we see in fire; and like fire, it does not tolerate admixture; and because it is not yet driven from its natural place it is not obliged to rise up again, but it revolves. By its action it shines, and by its power it gives warmth, yet it is in all respects of a nature that is very different from the nature of our fire.

After the heavenly fire, he posits a second type of fire, which gives warmth rather than light beneath the moon and which is called by the name of ether. A faint reflection of this is our own fire, which not only warms but even burns: it burns, I say, on account of its excessive admixture with earthy sharpness. But the fire which flourishes on fine material gives a purer light and a gentler warmth, especially when, having no constraints, it spreads out to its full extent.

To this he adds air, water, and earth. Yet he considers that every sphere of the world is composed of these five, so that there is among them all the fullest possible connection in substance and a total union in power and action. But he holds that within each sphere one of them is predominant and by its nature contains all the rest, too. Thus ether within earth is earthy, and earth within ether becomes ethereal; and it is the same in the sky. But there are more details on this subject in the *Theology* and in the commentaries to the *Timaeus*.

He accordingly places living, rational creatures in the sky, in the ether, in the air, in the water, and on earth. He says that these have been made by the soul: I mean, by the threefold soul. For he has it that beyond the single soul of the whole world there are the twelve souls of the twelve spheres. Then within each sphere there are twelve orders of souls. These orders are the constellations and stars in the sky, the human beings on earth, and the daemons in the upper ether, air, and water.

In each of these living beings the rational soul that is united to its own body creates a creature that is compounded from its own body and from life which has been directly imparted to the body. This life, which has now become corporeal, depends on a threefold soul: its own soul, the soul of the sphere, and the soul of the whole world. That the celestial realms have souls is deduced by Plato from the divine nature of heavenly substance, the extent it occupies, the life-giving power of its quality, and the speed and efficiency of movement in all things. Moreover, that celestial souls possess mind he conjectures from the order and constant nature of their movement.

He adds that there is the greatest possible necessity for soul to possess mind, and he understands this in two ways. The first way is to appreciate that the natural necessity, in this part of fire or in that, to consume and to rise up operates because it is guided from elsewhere, while the intellectual nature of the soul, insofar as it partakes of the intellect, is mistress of its own action. The second way is to appreciate that, since the movement of the soul is free by nature, it can easily go astray and, in turn, move about freely, unless it is regulated by the mind in its role as charioteer: I mean, by a mind which is mature and which considers in advance the best end of action and the most desirable way, right from the start.

Indeed, when this most noble mind is available to a most noble soul, as it is among the stars, then the task that is laid down is necessarily achieved; for bodies offer no resistance to the soul that is most noble, the soul with supreme power, and a mind full of nobility does not change its intention.

Hence he says that the three Fates maintain in perfection whatever the heavenly gods have decreed by their firm resolve. He speaks of three Fates or of a single Destiny which, in obedience to the nod of authority from divine minds, arranges three things: the beginnings, the intervening parts, and the ends of all things. But in an earlier book he says that those things determined by the decrees of fate are similar to wood that is prepared at the fire by being either straightened or twisted; for just as this wood can no longer be bent in another direction, so it is with regard to what has been decreed by fate. And it is not without justification that he mentions things that are rotated in relation to the fire, for the fiery spheres of the heavens are the instruments of fate.

Moreover, when he says that the stars are either eternal or very long-lived, he is clearly referring to the view expressed by Orpheus and perhaps by Hermes, which is that after many ages the world will be dissolved into fire. For every compound is ultimately subject to dissolution, and fire, the greatest and most powerful of all things, will, in an extraordinary way, eventually gather up all things into itself.

But the divine mind, the maker of this creation, will, with the slightest nod of assent, once more re-constitute from the fire a similar creation by means of a similar destiny.

This view was confirmed by Anaxagoras, Empedocles, Heraclitus, and many of the Stoics, all of whom declared that almighty God can preserve His handiwork for all time in the order imparted to it in a single action; but the work itself, being finite by nature and subject to internal strife, cannot be preserved. Yet God compensates with form whatever is deficient in form. Such is the vision of these men.

But as for you, you will observe at this point that Plato refutes those who deny that the heavenly bodies are alive on the grounds that they are always borne along in the same way. Indeed, the subject for everyone should be not the absence of life but the present abundance and wisdom.

Remember, moreover, that the soul is considered to be so different from the body that they have nothing in common, that is, they have no common substance. Again, because the soul does not depend on matter and because the bodily nature is deemed to be neither true substance nor true essence, he calls souls the gods of the stars, and he calls their bodies the images of the gods. So, then, among the celestial deities he calls Jove the gift of providence, and he calls Juno the life-giving power that is subordinate to providence. He also says that the stars are keenly perceptive of all things, through senses which are very different from ours.

He then describes the nature of daemons, which is endowed with prudence, sense perception, memory, and movement: a nature which is intermediate between gods and men; which is to be honoured for purposes of intercession and interpretation; and which is aware of our thoughts, favouring our good attitudes, movements, and emotions, whilst opposing the bad ones. He seems here to regard all daemons as good: all, that is, whom it is right to honour; but in other places he indicates that some are evil. He says that the ethereal daemons and the airy daemons are invisible, but that the watery daemons, whom he calls demi-gods, are visible, at times and with difficulty, but to the inner rather than the outer eye.

He adds that souls are prompted by daemons through dreams, voices, prophecies, and signs, but particularly at the time when the soul leaves the body. He says that religion has been much enhanced by these promptings. He also says that it is not lawful for mortal nature to change what has been established in religion by law, although it is lawful for the divine nature to do so.

Memorise this divine saying: The most divine principle of all has established the visible world, marvelling at which the fortunate man is fired by the love of his encounter with divinity and hence becomes blessed both in this life and in the next and, through wisdom which is truly one, he is also made truly one. Having been transported to realms which are in harmony with virtue, he is now ready to contemplate the divine for all remaining time.

The part of the translation which begins 'For divine matters' can be read elsewhere as 'For it is not proper for a reasonable man to honour some aspects of the divine and ignore others.'

At this point he intersperses some very well-known words about astronomy. He commends the quality of air which is moderated to the strength of one's temperament. Then, when he says that motion tending to the good starts its journey from the good soul, whereas motion ending in evil happens in the opposite way, do not think that there is a good world-soul and an evil world-soul, but consider that good things proceed from the world-soul insofar as it partakes of mind; otherwise, evils will come forth, that is, things completely devoid of the order of numbers. For he described evils earlier as those things which are devoid of harmonious number and beauty, whereas good things are those which are compounded of concordant numbers.

He adds that evils, lacking order, have been overcome by the good, by the Ideas of the divine mind, from the beginning of creation; that they need to be overcome as long as the world endures; and that these things have been said in accordance with the judgement which punishes the wicked, for the divine judgement which punishes the evil overcomes the evil of injustice with the goodness of justice.

You will note that religion is the highest virtue and that neglect of religion is the cause of wretched ignorance among men. Again, the best disposition is the one which is blended from temperance and courage: ready to learn, able to recall, and eager for things divine. And he says that when dispositions such as this have been rightly nurtured, the practice of religion spreads from them to others in the fullness of truth and is the most useful of all things to the State.

He says that wisdom cannot be learnt without God's help, but it would be better not to learn from someone who observes no measure in his teaching. He states that all things are so full of deities that the gods are not oblivious of our condition and do not withdraw their support from us.

But those things which he quickly touches upon concerning number we shall explain more fully at a more opportune moment. For the time being, receive a brief review. In themselves numbers are non-physical, being nothing other than repeated unity, which is indivisible. But as soon as they are considered to be allotted position, they can be thought of as being turned into points. Again, extension from one point to another gives birth to a line, from whose sweep is born a surface, from whose downward movement depth is produced. Some numbers are related to lines, some to surfaces, and others to cubes and solids. The first are binary, being as close as possible to unity. The second are quaternary, proceeding from unity by means of the binary. The third are octenary, coming from the binary doubled back upon itself.

Again, the perfect ratio is considered to be the double: firstly, because it is first, arising between one and two; secondly, because while it seems to have departed from the one it actually restores the one by doubling it; and thirdly, because it contains all other ratios, for the sesquialteral, the sesquitertial, and similar ratios are like parts beneath the double. Nature preserves this ratio in the heavens. On account of this ratio the sesquialteral preserves the sesquitertial: from these the double is composed.

For when the followers of Pythagoras measure the intervals between the spheres, they evaluate the Earth in relation to the Firmament and then in relation to the Moon and the Sun; and they evaluate the Sun, too, in relation to the Firmament. In these comparisons, the space between the Earth and the Sun, compared to the space between the Sun and the Firmament, makes a sesquialteral ratio between the Earth and the Sun; between the Sun and the Firmament it makes a sesqui-tertial ratio; and in that ratio is born the harmony of the diapente, from which, in turn, is born the diatessaron. From these two arise the double ratio and the harmony of the diapason. They believe that the space from the Earth to the Moon produces the diatessaron; the space from the Earth to the Sun produces the diapente; and the space from the Sun to the Firmament also produces the diatessaron.

But just as nature observes these ratios in the spheres, so, within the active and passive aspects of the elements, the agent must be twice as powerful as what is subordinate, in order for the action to be fulfilled. But why should this be so? It is because, since he is aiming at reduplicating himself through action, he undoubtedly has need of the reduplicating ratio. If, on the contrary, he covers less space, the resisting subordinate will prevent the fulfilment of the action. But just as the double ratio is conducive to the production of a substantial type, so the sesquialteral is conducive to the habitual condition and form of the type, while the sesquitertial is conducive to more general attributes.

Moreover, the measure of this kind of ratio is maintained in our humours; for they hold that there is twice as much blood as phlegm, twice as much phlegm as bile, and twice as much bile as black bile. If they have doubles, they consequently contain sesquialteral and sesquitertial ratios, which are within the double.

There are similar ratios in hearing, in which there are four levels of air, three of fire, two of water, and one of earth. Now, you know that between four and three there is the sesquitertial ratio, for four contains three and an additional unity, a third part of three. You also know that three is positioned between two and the sesquialteral ratio, for three contains two and one more unity, that is, half of two. This is why all the proportions are more evident in the condition of hearing than they are in the other conditions.

It is the same with harmony. The diapason, that is, the harmony of the eighth note, is in the double ratio. The diapente, that is, the harmony of the fifth note, is in the sesquialteral ratio. The diatessaron, that is, the harmony of the fourth note, is in the sesquitertial ratio.

I pass over the fact that similar ratios can be considered within the four elements: more of this elsewhere. The physicians agree on this and also on those matters which pertain to touch and, to some extent, to taste. They list four levels: the first is that which is scarcely perceived by the senses; the second is that which is clearly perceived but does not cause discomfort; the third is that which initially gives discomfort and then causes harm; the fourth is, in a word, destructive. In these four levels are found the double ratio, the sesquialteral and the sesquitertial, but it is the physician who understands these things.

At this point, Plato brings in one, two, four, six, eight, and twelve. From four to two there is the double, and from eight to four there is another double: indeed, these two additional quantities are proportionately equal, and each is produced by the double ratio, but they are not equal numerically, for eight is four more than four, and four is two more than two. Again, compare six firstly to four and then to eight: in comparison with four, there is the sesquialteral ratio, and in comparison with eight, there is the sequitertial ratio. These additional quantities are unequal proportionately, but are equal numerically; for in both cases the additional quantity is two. Next, compare six to twelve by the double proportion and then insert eight between them. Of course, between twelve and eight the sesquialteral ratio arises, and between eight and six there is the sesquitertial: from these is consti- tuted the double between six and twelve, in which the two additional quantities are clearly seen to be unequal both proportionately and numerically. All these matters are dealt with more conveniently in the commentaries to the *Timaeus*.

INDEX